D1125806

Letters for Every Occasion

A Pastor's Sourcebook

Letters
for **Every**
Occasion

Thomas J. Tozer

Abingdon Press
Nashville

LETTERS FOR EVERY OCCASION: A PASTOR'S SOURCEBOOK

Copyright © 1992 by Abingdon Press

All rights reserved.
No part of this work may be reproduced or transmitted in any form or by
any means, electronic or mechanical, including photocopying and
recording, or by any information storage or retrieval system, except as
may be expressly permitted by the 1976 Copyright Act or in writing from
the publisher. Requests for permission should be addressed in writing to
Abingdon Press, 201 Eighth Avenue South, Nashville, TN 37203.

This book is printed on recycled, acid-free paper.

Library of Congress Cataloging-in-Publication Data

Tozer, Tom, 1945–
    Letters for every occasion : a pastor's sourcebook / Tom Tozer.
        p.   cm.
    ISBN 0-687-21424-6 (alk. paper)
    1. Church correspondence.   2. Clergy—Correspondence.   3. Form letters.
I. Title.
BV652.9.T68   1992
651.7'52'0242—dc20   91-31288
                                                                          CIP

Scripture quotations, except where noted, are from the New Revised Standard
Version of the Bible, copyright © 1989, by the Division of Christian Education of
the National Council of the Churches of Christ in the United States of America,
and are used by permission.

Scripture quotations noted KJV are from the King James or Authorized Version
of the Bible.

95 96 97 98 99 00 01 02—10 9 8 7 6

MANUFACTURED IN THE UNITED STATES OF AMERICA

To the Reverend C. P. Tozer, my dad,
a great preacher and pastor . . . and pal

Acknowledgments

Sources quoted or that were in other ways helpful include:

Grants in the Humanities: A Scholar's Guide to Funding Sources, by William E. Coleman, Neal-Schuman Publishers, Inc., New York, 1980 (for grant information in grant application letter).

The Macmillan Dictionary of Quotations, Macmillan, New York, 1987.

More Seasonings for Sermons, by Phil Barnhart, C.S.S. Publishing Co., 1985.

The New Dictionary of Thought, compiled by Tyron Edwards, D.D., Standard Book Co., 1961.

Points with Punch, by Dennis R. Fakes, C.S.S. Publishing Co., 1982.

Still More Seasonings for Sermons, by Phil Barnhart, C.S.S. Publishing Co., 1986.

The Wonder of Words, by Edward Chinn, C.S.S. Publishing Co., 1985.

Contents

This model letter collection for pastors is the result, in part, of a survey of pastors across the country, representing Catholic and mainline Protestant denominations. In their judgment, these letters represent the most common subjects and events with which a majority of clergy must deal, at one time or another, in a caring, supportive, and sometimes delicate manner. In other words, you may never use all of the letters in this volume; and you certainly won't find every letter that you may need to write. However, all of you will use many of these letters; perhaps many of you will begin writing more pastoral letters than ever before!

Most pastors are better-than-average writers. These letters aren't necessarily an attempt to teach creative letter writing. But pastors are people, too. Not every "powerhouse in the pulpit" is a great wordsmith. And not every good wordsmith, clergy or otherwise, has the time to craft a letter for every deserving person or occasion— despite good intentions. (And yet, how much a few well-timed words can mean to someone!) This collection, therefore, is a hands-on reference for the busy pastor-preacher who also wants and strives to be an effective, "in touch" counselor and spiritual caregiver of his or her parish.

It is assumed that few of these letters will be reproduced word for word. Moreover, you are encouraged to adapt, amend, and expand upon them as you see fit, according to your needs and circumstances. Some letters may require very few changes. Others may need more development. Use these letters as you might a worship or preaching workbook—as a guide, leading you to and eliciting from you your own sentiments, style, and approach.

I have chosen not to include a few potential letters, because I do not believe that they should be letters at all. In matters relating to church staff differences, terminations, discussions of salaries and benefits, and the

Introduction

like, I would hope that those would be dealt with face-to-face, personally and confidentially. It is my feeling, and the feeling of many clergy, that when letters are substituted for in-person confrontations in matters relating to highly sensitive inter-staff issues, it merely increases the distance between parties. The discerning church professional and layperson will know when a letter is either insufficient or inappropriate.

No matter how you use the letters in this collection, I encourage you to use them generously. When I was in college, I was fortunate enough to win some writing and speaking awards. Several persons wrote me congratulatory notes. For whatever reason, my pastor didn't. Years later, when I found myself out of a job, I could have used a few comforting words from my pastor to carry with me. I could have, but . . .

On the positive side, I remember how appreciative (and truly impressed) my wife and I were when we received a personal note from the pastor of a church we visited while on vacation. We would probably never see one another again—the chances of our returning to that church were virtually nonexistent. Yet, that fine fellow took the time, with just a few words on paper, to make that special connection. And indeed, years later, we still feel warmly connected with him and that church.

I encourage you to make those wonderful, indelible connections!

Tom Tozer

Aldersgate United Methodist Church

23 West Crescent Blvd., Denton, Any State 77443
Phone: (173) 555-4323

Dear . . .

On behalf of the congregation at Aldersgate United Methodist Church, I would like to express our delight at your being with us in morning worship last Sunday.

Although we are far from your familiar surroundings, please make Aldersgate your spiritual resting place if you are ever again in our area.

You are always welcome here.

In Christ,

Pastor Johnson

Thank-You Letters

Christ Church

2010 Rural Hill Road
Standing Stone, Any State 12345
(155)-555-1098

Dear . . .

Someone once suggested that occasional visits—short and far between—are still very special . . . like those of angels.

It's always good to see you in Sunday morning worship. No matter how infrequent your visits to Christ Church, you remain in our thoughts and prayers. You are special to this church.

Please worship with us whenever you can.

God's blessings upon you.

Pastor Johnson

TRINITY CHURCH

9005 WEST PARK AVENUE   POUGHKEEPSIE, ANY STATE
00225
PHONE: (102)555-6744

Dear . . .

How delighted we were to have you and your lovely family with us last Sunday. Certainly it must have felt a little like coming home.

I am the fortunate benefactor of your good work here. This church is a wonderful, vibrant community of believers. It is a tribute to their abundant love and kindness that both you and I have felt good about being here.

Please come back any time.

With gratitude and blessings,

Pastor Johnson

Calvary Church of Christ

Calvary Church of Christ
Calvary Church of Christ

One Windsor Commons   Green Hills,   Any State   23118   (178) 555-9999

Dear . . .

On behalf of all members of Calvary Church of Christ, I would like to thank you for sharing your valuable time with us last Sunday.

As you know, parish life can become a little stale and stodgy. Sometimes our comfort turns to complacence. Your presence lifted our spirits and encouraged us to reach beyond our grasp. You radiate love and energy. That is evident in the renewed excitement I see and feel in our people since your visit.

May God bless your continued good work. And please don't wait for an invitation to come back!

In Christ,

Richard Johnson

Faith Brethren Church

**776 Willowbrook Road   Cumberland,
Any State   34567 (165)555-5643**

Dear . . .

Well done, good and faithful servant!

We at Faith Brethren Church are in your debt for your words of wisdom that you shared with us this past Sunday. Although your stay was brief, your presence lingers in heart and spirit.

You have done us all a great favor. Through the freshness and power of your unique perspective, you have infused us with renewed purpose and commitment. Our ministry here has been enriched and deepened. Thank you for that gift.

Bless you as you continue to inspire those whom you touch.

In Christ,

Pastor Johnson

St. John's Community Church

5008 Wilkerson Avenue
Nashville, Any State 30662 (150)555-3057

Dear . . .

Your contribution of (song/music) in last Sunday's worship service brought to mind a couple of lines from the poem "The Lotos-Eaters," by Alfred Lord Tennyson:

> Music that gentlier on the spirit lies,
> Than tir'd eyelids upon tir'd eyes.

Your (singing/music) was balm for the spirit. You have been gifted by God with an extraordinary talent. Thank you for sharing your precious gift with us. We are richer for it.

May God continue to guide and bless your life as you celebrate his love through (song/music).

In Christ,

Pastor Johnson

CENTRAL BAPTIST CHURCH

Route 66   Longville,   Any State   98989
(111)555-3879

Dear...

Repetition can be a great deadener. Sometimes worship falls into that deadly rut, losing its freshness and excitement.

Your participation last Sunday went a long way in keeping our worship experience what it ought to be—an occasion for celebration. It may be inappropriate to call it a party and yell "Surprise!" However, your contribution created a festive spirit and made it a very special morning!

I hope that we may call upon your talents again. Thank you for sharing *you!*

In Christ,

Pastor Johnson

Emmanuel
Lutheran
Church

107 Brook Dr.

Bethay

Any State
45789

(199)555-6811

Dear . . .

First, let me remind you of how grateful we are for your time, energy, and dedication in teaching our youngsters on Sunday morning. We do not acknowledge your contributions often enough. Your presence is a reminder that we should never take for granted our greatest resource—our teachers.

Second, during those times when you may feel overworked and under-appreciated, please remember this—what you do and say in your classroom may make the most important and lasting impression on a child's life that anyone will ever make in his or her lifetime. You may never know how or when you'll touch a young life. Years may pass before the spiritual seed you planted springs to fruition. Be assured, however, that you do touch the lives of our kids—and you have already made a significant difference.

Because of that, all of us—children, parents, the church—are in your eternal debt.

Thank you for teaching us.

In Christ,

Pastor Johnson

Good Shepherd
Community Church

968 Honeysuckle Road
Breezeville,   Any State   05050
Phone: (101)555-5467

Dear . . .

British humorist W. C. Sellar once remarked, "For every person wishing to teach there are thirty not wanting to be taught."

With that in mind, I want to thank you for the time you give to teaching our adults on Sunday morning. I know what a challenge it can be to corral a group of independent-thinking (even downright stubborn!) adults and to create an open atmosphere of sharing, caring, learning, and loving.

Yours is not an easy task. I must tell you, however, that it is a task that very few people are able to carry out with your degree of skill and aplomb. Thank you for tackling a tough assignment in our church, and for opening our eyes and minds to other perspectives.

Indeed, there are some among us who don't think they have anything new to learn . . . *but wouldn't miss your class for anything!*

Keep it up! You're terrific! And we're grateful!

In Christ,

Pastor Johnson

Dear . . .

You know, it still amazes me that it's always the people who are the busiest who manage to find the time to squeeze one more thing into their lives. Maybe it's because they truly see their talents as gifts from God.

You're one of those gifted people whose talent for leadership has made this year's (VBS or other program) an enriching experience for everyone involved.

We all have good intentions. But few of us are able to give those good intentions form and substance, because we lack the gifts of organization and leadership. It takes a special individual.

Thank God for your "specialness." And thank you for making this year's program so special!

In Christ,

Pastor Johnson

Christ Church

2010 Rural Hill Road
Standing Stone, Any State 12345
(155)555-1098

Dear . . .

Thank you for heading up the committee on
_____ (or, for heading up the _____ project). It
isn't easy to lead. Sometimes you have to stand
back and give others the reins of responsibility.
Occasionally you have to look on from the wings
and let the minor players take the bows.

Knowing when to lead and when to follow,
when to pass the torch or keep it—knowing how
to nurture others and recognize their contributions—all of these are attributes of an affirming,
caring, and most able leader. As (committee/proj-
ect) leader, you have done a fine job!

Thanks for doing what you do so very well.

In Christ,

Pastor Johnson

Dear . . .

Wow! Since you've been here, I know *where* things are, *when* things are, *how long* things are—even *why* things are! How did I manage before?

Things may become so organized around here that I'll have time for a few more rounds of golf! (Do you caddie? I could use some help finding my golf balls . . . Lord only knows where I might hit one!)

Thanks for being here. All of us appreciate your fine work.

Gratefully yours,

Pastor Johnson

Calvary Church of Christ

One Windsor Commons   Green Hills,   Any State   23118   (178)555-9999

Dear . . .

Thank you! Thank you! Thank you! I could fill this page with "Thank yous" and still owe you for all those times I have failed to say it. I'm sure others around here feel the same way.

There's no way to adequately acknowledge all that you do here at Calvary Church of Christ—both the quantity and quality of your work. What we can do (and should do more often) is to pause occasionally and express our sincere appreciation for your tireless efforts, your incredible patience, and your unceasing dedication—not to mention your top-notch administrative skills!

Because you help all of us do our jobs better, you play a vital role in the ministry of Calvary Church of Christ and in the mission of Christ's Church.

Thank you! Thank you! Thank you!

Richard Johnson

Faith Brethren Church

776 Willowbrook Road   Cumberland,
Any State   34567 (165)555-5643

Dear . . .

I want personally to thank you for your service
to me and to Faith Brethren Church these past
_____ years. You have been a good and faithful
servant in both administrative responsibilities and
matters of the spirit. You have been a model of one
whose desire was not to be served, but to serve.

Thank you for your dedication and commitment, on behalf of all of us who have been
touched by your life and have walked with you
into light.

God bless you as you continue to serve by your
example.

In Christ's name,

Pastor Johnson

St. John's Community Church

5008 Wilkerson Avenue
Nashville, Any State 30662 (150)555-3057

Dear...

I would like to take this opportunity to thank you personally for your gift to the St. John's Memorial Fund, in special tribute to the memory of
_____.

I believe that the Memorial Fund is the church's precious keepsake. Its value and meaning transcend mere dollars and cents. Inherent in a gift such as yours are the wonderful memories of a loved one—someone who inspired all of us to live in greater faith and to walk in the light of God's grace.

Your gift ensures that the legacy of _____ will live on. Thank you for entrusting St. John's Community Church with this memorial keepsake.

God's blessings upon your life.

Pastor Johnson

CENTRAL BAPTIST CHURCH

Route 66   Longville,   Any State   98989
(111)555-3879

Dear . . .

Just a brief note to express my personal gratitude to you for your financial support of the _____ (fund/project).

It is because of generous contributions like yours that we are able to broaden the scope of our ministry to include those who are often overlooked or forgotten. You are to be commended for your kindness.

May your gift be returned to you in the form of God's abundant blessings!

Thank you.

In Christ,

Pastor Johnson

Emmanuel Lutheran Church

107 Brook Dr.

Bethay

Any State 45789

(199)555-6811

Dear . . .

I would like to take this opportunity to thank you for making (renewing) your financial pledge to Emmanuel Lutheran Church.

Certainly all of us are the embodiment of Christ's Church regardless of matters of dollars and cents. Your financial pledge, however, goes a long way in supporting the programs here at Emmanuel, which otherwise would not be as effective or all-encompassing.

You will see your pledge at work in our church school program. You will see your pledge at work in our community. You may see some of your dollars patch a hole in our roof . . . or in someone's life. Whatever the need—practical or personal— your financial covenant to Emmanuel Lutheran Church will help meet it.

Thank you again for your gift. And please, remember Emmanuel Lutheran Church—its people, its pastor, and its mission—in your daily prayers.

In Christ's name,

Pastor Johnson

Good Shepherd Community Church

968 Honeysuckle Road
Breezeville, Any State 05050
Phone: (101)555-5467

Dear . . .

I am so very proud of you for the spirit of giving you demonstrated in our efforts to help the needy in our community. God bless you!

As concerned Christians, we sometimes look beyond the shores of our country to extend a helping hand, and in so doing, overlook the need right here in our own neighborhood. Your generosity is an example of putting Christianity to work for others, with no conditions or strings attached. Just a lot of love.

Truly we have been reminded that the joy is simply in the giving! Thank you for being such a giving church family!

In gratitude,

Pastor Johnson

Aldersgate United Methodist Church

23 West Crescent Blvd., Denton, Any State 77443
Phone: (173)555-4323

Dear...

On behalf of my family, I would like to thank you for the _____. Your kindness and generosity are most appreciated.

However, your greatest gift comes to us time and time again—your friendship, wrapped in warmth and laughter and love. You cannot do better than that!

We look forward to many more wonderful moments with you.

Thank you again. God bless you all.

Pastor Johnson

Christ Church

2010 Rural Hill Road
Standing Stone, Any State 12345
(155)555-1098

Dear . . .

Contrary to the beliefs of some, pastors are not made of steel. We can't always come to the rescue. We don't always have the answers. Sometimes we don't feel like smiling—or even being nice. It gets lonely atop this pedestal of impossible expectations. And try as we might, it's darn hard to climb down.

That's why I sincerely appreciated your allowing me to "come down" for just a while and bend your ear. It isn't often that a pastor can become just a person for a time—and unload on someone else.

It isn't often—but it sure does help. Thank you for listening.

Your friend in Christ,

Pastor Johnson

TRINITY CHURCH

9005 WEST PARK AVENUE   POUGHKEEPSIE, ANY STATE
00225
PHONE: (102)555-6744

Dear . . .

If our church had its own Chamber of Commerce or Welcome Wagon, you'd most certainly be a member! I say that because of the special position of leadership that you so deservedly hold in our church. I appreciate your efforts at making new members feel at home here. People never forget that first friendly smile or word of welcome.

Let me just encourage you to continue in the valuable role as an outreach person to new members. The job requires many hats, and you wear them all well: host, tour guide, traffic director, promoter, and caring friend.

As we attract more new folks to Trinity Church, your special people skills will be essential to our ministry and growth. Thank you for the good job you do. Keep it up!

Gratefully yours,

Pastor Johnson

A Letter to Write . . . and Then Shred!

Dear Boys in the Balcony . . .

Do your parents have any children who lived? The next time you obnoxious hooligans throw a paper plane from the balcony during my pastoral prayer, I'm gonna ask God to curse you with a seven-year plague of pimples! Last Sunday you nearly put Mrs. Neiman's eye out! Given the fact that she only has one eye, that could've been disastrous! What possessed you to stick a pin in the tip of that paper missile? That may very well be a crime—you're lucky she's too senile to sue you!

Look, I know you guys are bored to tears up there, but it's high time you realize that not everything in life is a game! Beginning next Sunday, I will thank you in advance (and from the depths of my palpitating heart) to get serious, grow up, and stop having so much fun on Sunday morning! You don't see anyone else having a good time, do you?

Your miffed minister,

Pastor Johnson

Calvary Church of Christ

One Windsor Commons   Green Hills,   Any State   23118   (178)555-9999

Dear . . .

There are no words to express my heartfelt sorrow for the death of _____. I can only offer you some comfort with these words from the Gospel of John, chapter 5:24:

Very truly, I tell you, anyone who hears my word and believes him who sent me has eternal life, and does not come under judgment, but has passed from death to life.

_____ was young and just beginning to form (his/her) own relationship with God. But (he/she) was fortunate to have parents who laid the foundation upon which (he/she) would build and shape (his/her) spiritual life. _____ believed because you believe. _____ knew God because you know God. At this moment, _____ possesses an understanding of God that none of us here can come close to imagining. I believe that with all my heart. You must believe it, too. For it is that belief that sustains our faith through the most difficult of times.

Please accept my condolences. I am here whenever you need me. Your church is here, too, to love and support you through this saddest of times.

You are in our prayers.

Richard Johnson

Letters of Condolence / Support / Encouragement

Faith Brethren Church

776 Willowbrook Road   Cumberland,
Any State   34567 (165)555-5643

Dear . . .

There are no words that will ease your pain just now. As your pastor, I can only offer you the promise that God offers each of us—the assurance that _____ is now in the embrace of our heavenly Father.

John 5:24 says;

> Very truly, I tell you, anyone who hears my word and believes him who sent me has eternal life, and does not come under judgment, but has passed from death to life.

_____ was a "hearer" and a "believer" of the Word. At this moment, (he/she) enjoys an understanding of God that you and I cannot even imagine. Please take comfort in knowing that.

As your friend, I am here for you whenever you need me. I offer a comforting hand or shoulder or ear and as much time as you want. Please don't hesitate to ask me.

Your church is here, too, to love and support you during this saddest of times. Lean on us.

Most of all, hold firm in your faith—as you and _____ have done together for so many years.

You are in our prayers.

Pastor Johnson

St. John's Community Church

5008 Wilkerson Avenue
Nashville, Any State 30662 (150)555-3057

Dear . . .

This is probably a difficult time for you. A year is hardly long enough to heal the wound of _____'s passing. I want you to know that you are in my prayers right now. I am asking God to continue to give you the strength to get through this difficult time.

Memories of _____ linger in the minds of all of us who knew and loved (him/her). We are all better people for having known (him/her). If heaven can be more heavenly, it already is! After all, _____'s been there a year!

Please let me know if I can be of any help right now. Otherwise, I will understand your need for solitude and reflection.

Christ walks with you.

Pastor Johnson

CENTRAL BAPTIST CHURCH

Route 66   Longville,   Any State   98989
(111)555-3879

Dear . . .

Please accept my heartfelt condolences on the death of your (mother/father). I offer my prayers that you will find the strength to sustain you through your pain and sorrow.

Someone once said, upon the death of a loved one, "God finally caught his eye."

Your (mother/father) was God's good and faithful servant. Always active. Deeply devoted. Sincere in every word and deed. God finally caught (her/his) eye and beckoned (her/him) home for a well-deserved, eternal rest.

May you find comfort in knowing that your (mother/father) now walks and talks with God.

You are in our prayers.

Pastor Johnson

Emmanuel Lutheran Church

107 Brook Dr.

Bethay

Any State 45789

(199)555-6811

Dear . . .

I want you to know how very sorry I am to hear about the death of _____.

It's hard to understand why things have to die. Even we grown-ups don't know the reasons why. There are some things in life that make us sad— and the death of a good friend makes us very sad.

But you know what? I'd like you to remember all the fun you had with _____. And I hope you'll thank God for giving you and _____ those special times together. God is also sorry that _____ isn't here anymore, but he's glad that you and _____ were such great friends.

God is your friend, too, _____. He's with you right now while you're sad. And he'll be with you when you're happy again.

We'll all miss _____. (He/She) was a good pal.

Your friend,

Pastor Johnson

Good Shepherd Community Church

968 Honeysuckle Road
Breezeville,   Any State   05050
Phone: (101)555-5467

Dear . . .

The death of a companion is always painful—especially one such as _____, who brought you so much joy.

Your grief is understandable and necessary. As difficult as it may be just now, however, please try to remember with joy and gratitude the life you shared together. So many people spend their entire lives without experiencing a loving, trusting relationship. Your life has been enriched!

_____ was truly one of God's blessings in your life. Please accept my sympathy for your loss.

In Christ,

Pastor Johnson

Dear . . .

I am so sorry to hear the news about your business. I have never owned a business, but I can imagine that losing it must be like losing part of yourself. So much of your heart and soul goes into it that when the worst happens, you must feel at once hurt and angry and empty.

May God give you the strength to get through this difficult time.

> Be strong and bold; have no fear or dread of them, because it is the Lord your God who goes with you; he will not fail you or forsake you.
> (Deuteronomy 31:6)

Your pastor and your church are here whenever you need us. Please let us know what we can do to help. We love you. We want to help if we can.

In Christ,

Pastor Johnson

Christ Church

2010 Rural Hill Road
Standing Stone, Any State 12345
(155)555-1098

Dear . . .

I am so sorry to hear about your recent job loss. In spite of the anger or hurt that you may be feeling right now, I urge you to hold fast to your faith.

We shake our heads in disbelief and wonder why these things have to happen. I believe that it helps to view these apparent misfortunes as new opportunities, fresh starts, open doors to spiritual growth and maturity.

I also believe that if our faith means anything, then we must keep it strong during the toughest of times. The alternative is despair—and God expects our response to be nobler and more self-affirming than that.

Right now, ask God for strength and direction, and then be ready for a new and exciting chapter in your life! Your pastor and your church will help you fight the good fight of faith all the way!

Be strong and keep the faith!

Pastor Johnson

TRINITY CHURCH

9005 WEST PARK AVENUE   POUGHKEEPSIE, ANY STATE
00225
PHONE: (102)555-6744

Dear . . .

What you may need right now more than anything is a non-judgmental friend who will listen while you lean on (him/her). I would like to be that friend and shoulder, if you wish.

I can't know exactly how you feel, because I am not in your shoes. However, I would imagine you must be going through a blur of emotions—anger, hurt, sadness, loneliness, perhaps even relief. All of these feelings are very human and natural. Allow yourself to feel them, and in so doing, the healing will begin.

Ask God for direction right now and be open to him. Though it would be natural for you to deny his presence during this painful time, be assured that he has not abandoned you. He is your constant source of strength during the best and worst of times.

My prayers are with you and _____ (spouse). It is my hope that both of you will gain personal insight and wisdom from this sad experience. Your pastor and church are here to share your burden, when you are ready.

God is with you.

Pastor Johnson

Calvary Church of Christ

Calvary Church of Christ
Calvary Church of Christ

One Windsor Commons   Green Hills,   Any State   23118   (178)555-9999

Dear . . .

I am so sorry for the strained relations between you and _____ (name of son/daughter). It is very difficult for those of us who are not in your situation to offer you just the right words of support or comfort. And yet, because we love you, we must try.

Schopenhauer, the German philosopher, said: "Every parting gives a foretaste of death; every coming together again a foretaste of the resurrection."

We offer you our prayers during these difficult days. We will pray for the time when you and _____ come back together on a higher plane of love and understanding—your relationship repaired and resurrected.

May the Lord be with you both.

In Christ's love and keeping,

Richard Johnson

Faith Brethren Church

776 Willowbrook Road   Cumberland,
Any State   34567 (165)555-5643

Dear . . .

This is just to let you know how sorry I am for your recent mishap. I—indeed all of us—are praying for your speedy and complete recovery.

In the meantime, call upon us if there is anything we can do to help keep your life in order while your body is slightly out of order. Cook? Clean? Shop? Taxi? Your command is our wish. Just ask.

Get well. We love you.

In Christ,

Pastor Johnson

St. John's Community Church

5008 Wilkerson Avenue
Nashville, Any State 30662 (150)555-3057

Dear . . .

I want you to know you are in my constant prayer of appeal that God will heal your body and restore your spirit. I don't know just how much pull I have with God, but I have made it clear in no uncertain terms that we need you *here!*

The most important thing for you right now is not to lose heart. Be strong. Be unafraid. Be at peace.

Whatever God's will be for you, take comfort in knowing that God's greatest gift is eternal *life.*

The Lord make his face to shine upon you and give you peace.

We love you.

Pastor Johnson

CENTRAL BAPTIST CHURCH

Route 66   Longville,   Any State   98989
(111)555-3879

Dear . . .

Sometimes we pastors are accused of sticking our noses in where they don't belong. So I'm leaving my nose at home and am sending you these words instead.

It's so easy to fall back on cliches. Cheer up, the sun will shine tomorrow! Into everyone's life some rain must fall! Things could always be worse! But it's much more difficult to say . . . I don't know quite what to say. I have no instant pain reliever—no miracle cure for heartache.

But . . . I can offer my hand for comfort and support. And you're invited to take it whenever you want. I will respect your wish to be alone right now—but my hand is here.

You are in my prayers. And you are in God's care.

Pastor Johnson

Emmanuel
Lutheran
Church

107 Brook Dr.

Bethay

Any State
45789

(199)555-6811

Dear ...

What a time of mixed emotions this holiday season must be for you. Certainly it is a time to celebrate the birth of our Lord and Savior, Jesus Christ. However, because of the death of your beloved _____, this will also be a season of solemn reflection for you—and for all of us who miss (her/him).

I am asking God to help you get through this season. And in spite of your understandable sadness, may we all rejoice in our Lord Jesus Christ, whose birth was the promise of eternal life for all who believe in him! _____ believed in him with all (her/his) heart. And now (she/he) knows the eternal peace that passes all understanding. There is great joy in that!

May God bless you this season.

Pastor Johnson

Good Shepherd Community Church

968 Honeysuckle Road
Breezeville, Any State 05050
Phone: (101)555-5467

Dear...

Just a brief note to extend my thoughts and prayers to your family as you prepare to send _____ off to _____. This is at once the ending and the beginning of an era. It is a happy, sad, anxious time for everyone.

You have provided a good Christian home for _____. You have given (her/him) all the right tools to make it on (her/his) own, with God's guiding hand. Take comfort in knowing that you have done your best as parents to prepare _____ for what lies ahead.

Now you must let go and allow (her/him) to stumble, fall, learn, grow, and fly! Bless you all as you begin new and exciting lives in God's loving care.

In Christ,

Pastor Johnson

A Letter to Write ... and Then Shred!

Dearly Beloved Committee Member . . .

I am writing to express my regret at the failure of your idea to meet with committee approval last evening. But honestly, it was the dumbest idea I've ever heard of. The kindest thing we could do was to put it out of its misery.

You always have so much to share at these meetings, so many suggestions about how to do everything—but you never support them with clear thinking, organization, or vision. What you say is nearly always (no, *always*) warmed over, half-baked, or totally fried! You shoot from the lip and always hit your foot! Of course, they both adorn that wind tunnel under your nose! Why, you couldn't hit the side of a barn with a clear point if you were standing inside it!

Look, I don't mean to hurt your feelings . . . I mean to *shut you up!*

The only thing left is to give your idea a decent burial. It'll have lots of company.

Rest in peace . . . and quiet . . . *puhleeeeezzzzze!*

Passionately and compassionately yours,

Pastor Johnson

Dear . . .

A year ago I was privileged to officiate at the wedding of two very special people. It hardly seems possible, does it? And yet, here it is, your first anniversary!

I want you both to know how proud I am to have shared in the most important moments of your lives. I can recall the love in your eyes that day. That sparkle is still there. Thank you for your example of love and commitment—and congratulations on #1!

(Now that you're no longer newlyweds, you can really let your hair down! Ha!)

God bless your marriage.

In Christ,

Pastor Johnson

Christ Church

2010 Rural Hill Road
Standing Stone, Any State 12345
(155)555-1098

Dear . . .

My hearty congratulations to you both for reaching that marital milestone of fifty years together! Wow!

In this day and age of unsettledness, I am grateful for the example you two set for the younger couples in our parish of a loving, lasting commitment to each other.

Most of us experience rough times in the best of marriages. Some of us sound a hasty retreat as soon as things don't meet our selfish expectations. You two remind us all that it is possible to weather the storms of married life together and come through stronger than ever!

Congratulations on your first fifty years! May God continue to bless your beautiful union.

In Christ,

Pastor Johnson

TRINITY CHURCH

9005 WEST PARK AVENUE   POUGHKEEPSIE, ANY STATE
00225
PHONE: (102)555-6744

Dear . . .

Congratulations! This is truly a time of joy and celebration in the _____ household!

May God bless you as you welcome this new life into your family. The writer James Baldwin once wrote, "Children have never been very good at listening to their elders, but they have never failed to imitate them."

As you well know, along with your new bundle of joy comes a bundle of responsibility. Your child will watch you and learn from you. You will be (his/her) entire world for many months to come. Your every word and gesture and expression will be (his/her) "classroom." I encourage you to keep God as the cornerstone of your home and family. In doing that, you will grow together in love and respect.

Thanks be to God for richly blessing your lives. May your family grow with God.

In Christ,

Pastor Johnson

Calvary Church of Christ

Calvary Church of Christ
Calvary Church of Christ

One Windsor Commons   Green Hills,   Any State   23118   (178)555-9999

Dear . . .

No doubt you've been swamped with congratulatory calls and letters. I just want to take a moment to express my own personal happiness for you and your new (son/daughter). I have always felt that we come as close to seeing God as we ever shall when we experience the wonder of birth.

I encourage you to let your new (son/daughter) experience God's love in your home. Your baby will experience that love in the way you look, touch, and speak to (him/her). Your baby will come to know God through you. That's a wonderful and awesome responsibility.

Bless you as you begin the greatest adventure life has to offer. May God continue to give you strength and guidance in the challenging, demanding months ahead.

Congratulations!

Best wishes,

Richard Johnson

Faith Brethren Church

**776 Willowbrook Road   Cumberland,
Any State   34567   (165)555-5643**

Dear . . .

Congratulations on the birth of your new (son/daughter). I have often thought that we come as close to seeing God as we ever shall when we experience the miracle of birth.

Your (son/daughter) is fortunate to have such (loving parents/a loving parent). God resides in your home already. Because of that, your baby will see God's love in your eyes and feel God's love in your touch. Your baby will come to know God through you. That's a wonderful and awesome responsibility.

God bless your home. May you continue to nurture your children in the Christian faith. Your pastor and church pledge to help you in that effort.

In Christ,

Pastor Johnson

St. John's Community Church

5008 Wilkerson Avenue
Nashville, Any State 30662 (150)555-3057

Dear . . .

Your first grandchild! Does that make you feel older or younger? I know it makes you feel terrific!

God has blessed your family with the continuity that a new life promises. Your grandchild represents the richness of your past and the hope of your future.

Your influence will be great. In your eyes, (he/she) will see the peace and contentment of a God-centered life. In your voice, (he/she) will learn the sound of certainty and wisdom. In your arms, (he/she) will know the comfort of both gentleness and strength. From your grandchild's perspective, you will always have the time for the important things.

Congratulations! May your grandchild know and grow in God's love.

In Christ,

Pastor Johnson

CENTRAL BAPTIST CHURCH

Route 66   Longville,   Any State   98989
(111)555-3879

Dear . . .

"Great" certainly describes the occasion and the people involved! Congratulations! You're (a) new *great* grand (mother, father, parents) of a new *great* grand (son, daughter)! That's *great, great, great!*

It must give you great pleasure to see the torch of life passed on to newer generations in your family. May God continue to bless your life and the lives of those whom you have helped to nurture in his name.

Congratulations on your latest, *great* accomplishment!

Yours in celebration and joy,

Pastor Johnson

Dear . . .

Congratulations on your decision to have _____ baptized at the altar of Emmanuel Lutheran Church. In so doing, you have surrendered _____'s life to God's eternal care, supported and nurtured by your deep and abiding faith.

_____ is very young. We acknowledge that (he/she) has little understanding of this sacred occasion. We need to be reminded, therefore, that the rite of Holy Baptism is symbolic of our very real intentions to instill God's love in your child's life. This love must be taught through word and deed by you, (his/her) parents, and by us, your (son's/daughter's) church family. It is we who must ensure that this baptismal covenant with God is fulfilled.

May God help us all to be examples of his love in your (son's/daughter's) life.

God bless you in this important decision.

In Christ,

Pastor Johnson

Emmanuel
Lutheran
Church

107 Brook Dr.

Bethay

Any State
45789

(199)555-6811

Good Shepherd Community Church

968 Honeysuckle Road
Breezeville,   Any State   05050
Phone: (101)555-5467

Dear . . .

When you were _____ old, you were baptized at the altar of Good Shepherd Community Church. You were probably too young to remember it. Certainly you did not understand it.

In presenting you for baptism, your parents and church family promised God that they would bring you up in the Christian faith, teaching you through their love and example. You are now old enough to understand the full significance of this sacred occasion.

In Romans 6:4-6, Paul speaks of baptism. He says that by our being baptized, we rise with Christ into newness of life. We need not fear death. For it is through our death on earth that we are resurrected. It is Christ's victory over death that prepares a way for each of us to gain newness of life—for eternity.

In a way, your baptism at an early age was—and is—a victory cry! It is a celebration of your life with God in the center! And of life over death!

You are also old enough now to make your own conscious commitment to a God-centered life. You can make this commitment with others your age in our upcoming Confirmation class. The confirmation experience offers you the opportunity to "confirm" your baptism—to say yes to a God-filled life. It is a renewal of the covenant that your parents and church family made with God years ago. Now it is yours to make.

Confirmation class will begin on _____ . Please pray about your decision to participate. It is a serious decision, one that God wants you to consider carefully and thoughtfully.

May your thoughts and deeds always be God-centered.

In Christ,

Pastor Johnson

Dear . . .

Congratulations on your being baptized at the altar of Aldersgate United Methodist Church. You have made a covenant with God in which you promise to keep God at the center of your life.

In Romans 6:4-6, Paul says that by being baptized, we rise with Christ into the newness of life. We celebrate his resurrection just as we rejoice in our own victory over death!

May your God-centered life continue to be an inspiration to all of us and an example of the joy and perpetual newness of life through Christ!

God's blessings upon your life.

Pastor Johnson

Christ Church

2010 Rural Hill Road
Standing Stone, Any State 12345
(155)555-1098

Dear . . .

I would like to congratulate you on your recent award. To be especially good at something means a lot. It means you are willing to work hard to do the very best you can. That's important.

You know what? Some people live their entire lives and never do any more than to just get by. They just don't seem to care. Or maybe no one is around to give them a push or a pat on the back.

You're lucky to have people around you who encourage you. In a way, you're really sharing your award with them. Without their love and help, maybe you wouldn't have tried so hard.

Please share your award with God, too, will you? God created you with talent and skills. God gave you the tools to help you earn this honor. Remember to thank God the next time you say your prayers.

Congratulations again! We are happy for you and proud of you!

Your pastor,

The Reverend Johnson

TRINITY CHURCH

9005 WEST PARK AVENUE   POUGHKEEPSIE, ANY STATE
00225
PHONE: (102)555-6744

Dear . . .

I would like to extend my personal congratulations to you on your recent achievement. Your pastor and your church are extremely proud of you!

We need young people like you who aren't embarrassed or ashamed to set good examples for others. You would be surprised at how many children in our community may be looking at you right now in silent admiration. To them, you are bigger than life! They are lucky to have such a positive role model.

I wish you well in all your future endeavors. May this special recognition be only the beginning of many blessings to come your way. And may you continue to be open to God's guidance.

In Christ's service,

Pastor Johnson

Calvary Church of Christ

One Windsor Commons   Green Hills,   Any State   23118   (178)555-9999

Dear . . .

Robert Browning once wrote, "Ah, but a man's [person's] reach should exceed his grasp, Or what's a heaven for?" (from "Andrea del Sarto").

You have extended your reach beyond your grasp with your recent accomplishments. Congratulations on your courage to stretch yourself!

So many people never live up to their potential. It's a sad commentary on our society that we don't seem to put a premium on quality anymore, either of product or performance. We need people who aren't afraid to excel, who aren't embarrassed to be the very best they can be.

We need more people like you. It is my hope and prayer that your achievement will serve as encouragement to others whose talents remain hidden under a bush.

May God continue to bless you. *And stretch you.*

In Christ,

Richard Johnson

Faith Brethren Church

**776 Willowbrook Road   Cumberland,
Any State   34567 (165)555-5643**

Dear . . .

Congratulations on (joining/becoming a member of/becoming a part of)_____!

Getting involved. That's a phrase we give a lot of lip service to. But many people are afraid to really go for it! I'm glad that you're involved in _____. You will make a positive difference with your talents and abilities. The fact that you are participating just may inspire someone else to get with it!

May God continue to give you the courage to get involved—to share, to serve, and to make a difference.

In Christ,

Pastor Johnson

St. John's Community Church

5008 Wilkerson Avenue
Nashville, Any State 30662 (150)555-3057

Dear . . .

A new job can give you many things—butterflies in your stomach, sleepless nights, your own spending money. It can also provide you with the chance to prove yourself—to set new standards of excellence and quality. What a challenge to make your shoes so hard to fill that no one else but you can do your job!

View your new job as an opportunity to make your own mark of excellence. Jump in with both feet and learn all you can. Do such good work that when the time comes for you to leave, your boss won't know what to do without you!

Remember, your first job will be your most important recommendation for your next job. And your first boss will be a valuable reference down the road. Do your very best! Your church and your pastor are rooting for you!

Pray for God's guidance.

In Christ,

Pastor Johnson

CENTRAL BAPTIST CHURCH

Route 66   Longville,   Any State   98989
(111)555-3879

Dear...

I would like to extend my personal congratulations to you on your graduation from high school. I'm sure this is the first of many fine accomplishments to come in your life.

I'll bet you thought this day would never arrive. But here it is! Now you are at a crossroads in your life. Choices will come from all directions. You will be faced with some tough decisions.

Let God help you make the right decisions. Remember that God is by your side. Ask for guidance, and listen for directions. God will never abandon you.

Your church family is proud of your accomplishments. We will continue to love you and keep you in our prayers as you begin a new journey toward independence and maturity.

Grow with God.

Pastor Johnson

Emmanuel
Lutheran
Church

107 Brook Dr.

Bethay

Any State
45789

(199)555-681

Dear . . .

   Congratulations on your scholarship! I'm sure
your parents are proud of you. So are your church
and your pastor!
   A scholarship is a recognition of your abilities
and a reward for your hard work. Use it well, as
I'm sure you will. Others who come after you will
look upon you as an inspiration and a model to
follow. Sounds corny, but it's true.
   Thank God for this wonderful gift! You are truly
deserving and blessed. May God remain an important part of your promising future.

                    In Christ,

                    Pastor Johnson

Good Shepherd Community Church

968 Honeysuckle Road
Breezeville,   Any State   05050
Phone: (101)555-5467

Dear . . .

Congratulations on your recent job promotion! Consider this well-earned honor as God's opening a new door for you.

God opens doors to us for a reason. Sometimes it's hard to understand why. Sometimes we're afraid to go through them. Perhaps we don't feel we're ready or deserving. But God grants us opportunities when we are ready for a challenge, a change, or a stretch. Your promotion could be God's way of telling you that you have much more to give—that you've just begun to tap your potential. And you thought you had stopped growing!

Seize the opportunity. And ask God to lead the way as you tackle your new responsibilities.

You have done well!

In Christ,

Pastor Johnson

Dear . . .

Congratulations on your recent retirement from
_____. This must be a happy and sad time for
you. I'm sure you welcome the rest. You deserve
it. But I'm also sure it's hard to say goodbye to
coworkers and to a way of life for _____ years.

You've been a model of integrity and dedication
on the job, attributes that seem to be in short sup-
ply these days. You should be proud of your example and accomplishments. We are!

You've reached a new and unfamiliar crossroads in your life. If I can be of any help while you
consider your options and decide your next move,
please let me know. Knowing you as I do, retirement will not slow you down for long.

May God be with you during this time of transition.

In Christ,

Pastor Johnson

Christh Church

2010 Rural Hill Road
Standing Stone, Any State 12345
(155)555-1098

Dear . . .

I am writing to let you know how happy I am that you have found a new job. I know your search has been long and hard. But your persistence has paid off!

If they gave a medal for perseverance, you'd be wearing it. The past few months have been difficult for you and your family. I pray that you have kept your faith strong. It's hard to know why God sometimes tests us so severely—but I truly believe that God chooses "test-takers" with a larger plan in mind.

Keep you faith strong and your heart open to God's will. There may be more to this new opportunity than just another job!

Be ready.

Yours in Christ,

Pastor Johnson

A Letter to Write . . . and Then Shred!

Dear Organ Grinder . . .

Congratulations! You actually got through the entire worship service last Sunday without (a) rewriting a hymn; (b) hitting the keyboard with your elbow during my sermon; or (c) playing the fifth verse of a hymn of four verses! (My prayers are finally getting some attention.)

Look, I respect your talent. (It's a lonely position to have.) And I can accept the fact that musicians are a temperamental lot. But please don't sit there in a huff, all sour-pussed and slump-shouldered, every time the furnace fan kicks on during your prelude. More often than not, most of us find the whirring fan the more comforting of the two noises.

Cacophonously yours,

Pastor Johnson

TRINITY CHURCH

9005 WEST PARK AVENUE   POUGHKEEPSIE, ANY STATE
00225
PHONE: (102)555-6744

Dear . . .

I would like to wish you a happy 13th birthday. You are officially a teenager!

Someone once joked that old people believe everything, middle-aged people are suspicious of everything, and young people *know* everything! How does it feel to be so wise? Just kidding.

You have reached an important stage of your life. To you it probably has taken forever. Before you know it, however, you will look back on your teenage years and marvel at how time flies!

Your teens will be exciting years. They will also be filled with anxiety, confusion, frustration, temptation, and doubt. As you start down this wonderful and sometimes rough road, I want to assure you that God will be with you every step of the way. There will be times when you think God has forgotten you. Believe me when I say this is when you'll want to listen the hardest for God's guidance.

Congratulations on turning 13! Always remember to make God an important part of your teen years.

Your friend in Christ,

Pastor Johnson

Milestone Birthdays/Events

Calvary Church of Christ

Calvary Church of Christ
Calvary Church of Christ
Calvary Church of Christ

One Windsor Commons   Green Hills,   Any State   23118   (178)555-9999

Dear . . .

Congratulations on getting your driver's license! (I'll bet you thought the day would never come.) It is indeed a great privilege to be able to drive a car. I know you will treat it as such.

There is one driving rule that you won't find in an instruction booklet. It is found in Matthew 22, verse 39, and says, "Love your neighbor as yourself." We don't usually apply that important commandment to driving, but it's not a bad idea. All of us share the streets and highways. As Christians, we need to demonstrate our love for one another no matter where we are—behind the wheel or behind our desks.

Remember this. When you and I are on the road, I must trust you and you must trust me. Our lives and the lives of our loved ones are in each other's hands. That's an awesome responsibility.

Drive carefully, _____ (name). And again, congratulations on *finally* getting that license!

Your friend in Christ,

Richard Johnson

Faith Brethren Church

776 Willowbrook Road   Cumberland,
Any State   34567 (165)555-5643

Dear . . .

Twenty-one! Oh boy! Look out! What now?
Freedom! Whoopee!

Stop, look, and listen. Caution. Yield when necessary. Watch out for soft shoulders. Go slowly.

Be strong and firm. Stick to your guns. Shoot
straight with everyone. Make sure, when you face
yourself in the mirror tomorrow, you like what
you see.

Have a blast! Be kind, loving, compassionate,
and Christian.

Go with God.

Congratulations on being 21.

Your friend in Christ,

Pastor Johnson

St. John's Community Church

5008 Wilkerson Avenue
Nashville, Any State 30662 (150)555-3057

Dear . . .

Happy 30th birthday!

Hmm. Thirty. You're still kind of youthful, but no longer silly. And you're kind of older now, but you're far from decaying. You're sort of too young to be considered wise, but you're too old to be making unwise decisions. To many folks, you're still kind of a squirt. To yourself, I'll bet you sort of feel like you just hurdled the hill, fell off a cliff, and landed head-first in the valley of the shadow of death!

Thirty. Hmm. It's sort of a *sort of . . . kind of* age, isn't it . . . kind of?

Well, look at the bright side. Most people younger than you think they know it all and don't know anything. And most people older than you think they know everything, but they're starting to forget it!

You didn't know you were sort of so brilliant, did you? There. Feel better? Kind of?

Happy 30th!

Pastor Johnson

P.S. Think of yourself not as over the hill but as over the hump. It's all downhill now! (And it gets faster and faster!)

CENTRAL BAPTIST CHURCH

Route 66   Longville,   Any State   98989
(111)555-3879

Dear . . .

Happy 40th! Aw come on, it can't be that bad . . . can it?

You know what Bob Hope says? "Middle age is when your age starts to show around the middle." (Are you laughing? Crying? *Dieting?*)

Well, you know it had to come eventually. Now you're considered no longer young and yet not quite old. A little out of shape but not quite withering. Kind of over the hill, but with a few more mountains to climb!

Relax. The best is yet to come. American psychologist and author Walter B. Pitkin wrote a book called *Life Begins At Forty*. Here's what he said:

> You who are crossing forty may not know it, but you are the luckiest generation ever. Every day brings forth some new thing that adds to the joy of life after forty. Work becomes easy and brief. Play grows richer and longer. Leisure lengthens. Life's afternoon is brighter, warmer, full of song; and long before the shadows stretch, every fruit grows ripe.

How's that? Feel better? Well anyway, I want to extend my congratulations to you on achieving one of life's important milestones—and I wish you another, even happier forty years. I'm glad you have included God in your first forty.

A very blessed birthday to you, _____ (name).

Pastor Johnson

Emmanuel
Lutheran
Church

107 Brook Dr.

Bethay

Any State
45789

(199)555-6811

Dear . . .

Someone less sensitive than I would remind you that you have now reached the half-century mark—or that you are now considered a "semi-antique" by serious artifact collectors. Someone with no tact whatsoever would just start TALKING LOUDER AROUND YOU! How insensitive, indeed.

Seriously though, I wish you another fifty as good as and even better than your first fifty. Your life has served as an inspiration to all of us. Everyone who knows you considers that in itself a privilege!

Happy birthday, _____ (name). Thanks for being you. May God grant you continued health and happiness.

In Christ,

Pastor Johnson

Good Shepherd Community Church

968 Honeysuckle Road
Breezeville, Any State 05050
Phone: (101)555-5467

Dear . . .

I would like to extend my hearty congratulations to you on your 80th birthday! Happy, happy birthday!

You know, those of us who are still trying to sort out all of life's mysteries look to you for inspiration to carry on. We've come to depend on your empowering presence here at Good Shepherd Community Church. We look forward, in gratitude and reverence, to your continued warmth and light.

On behalf of your many friends and loved ones who span several generations, I want to thank you for sharing your life with us. For what you mean to us, we are in your eternal debt.

God bless you on your 80th birthday!

In Christ,

Pastor Johnson

Dear . . .

Things of quality endure forever—including people like you!

Happy 100th birthday! It is truly an honor to be able to congratulate you on your remarkable achievement. Some would say you had nothing to do with it, that it just happened naturally. But I wonder. I have a feeling that your good heart and steadfast trust in God have sustained you over these many years.

Thank you for showing us that the Fountain of Youth can be discovered at any age—that growing old need not wrinkle a person's spirit. You are an inspiration to all of us.

God bless your old age and your youth!

Happy, happy birthday!

In Christ,

Pastor Johnson

A Letter to Write . . . and Then Shred!

Dear Worshiper . . .

Regrettably, we are canceling this year's special foot-washing ceremony. Too many parishioners felt that this type of worship celebration would just be too humiliating an experience.

Yours in humility,

Pastor Johnson

P.S. In other words, everyone got cold feet! Poor soles.

Christ Church

2010 Rural Hill Road
Standing Stone, Any State 12345
(155)555-1098

Dear . . .

Thank you for inviting me to speak at _____. I would be only too happy to accept and would welcome your guidance as to the specific focus and length of my address.

Woodrow Wilson once remarked upon receiving an invitation to make a speech, "If you want me to talk for ten minutes I'll come next week. If you want me to talk for an hour I'll come tonight."

As soon as you fill me in on the particulars, I'll begin rehearsing immediately. By the time I see you, my speech should be just long enough to cover the subject and short enough to endear myself to your audience!

Let me hear from you. And thanks again. I am truly honored.

Respectfully yours,

Pastor Johnson

TRINITY CHURCH

9005 WEST PARK AVENUE   POUGHKEEPSIE, ANY STATE
00225
PHONE: (102)555-6744

Dear . . .

Thank you for your kind invitation to speak at
_____. Under ordinary circumstances, I would
be happy to accept. Unfortunately, I have another
commitment on that day (evening), which forces
me to decline this fine opportunity.

I am sure this will be a very special occasion. I
extend my wishes to you for a rousing success.
And please, keep me in mind for a future engage-
ment should you require a speaker. I would be
honored.

Regretfully and graciously yours,

Pastor Johnson

Calvary Church of Christ

One Windsor Commons   Green Hills,   Any State   23118   (178)555-9999

Dear . . .

Thank you again for accepting (my/our) invitation to speak at Calvary Church of Christ on _____ (date) at _____ (time). We look forward to your arrival with great joy.

If you need additional information (or if my directions to the church are hopelessly muddled!), please give me a call. Otherwise, I will look forward to seeing you on _____ (date).

In Christ,

Richard Johnson

P.S. If you're able to be here half an hour or so early, we'll go over any last-minute details.

Faith Brethren Church

**776 Willowbrook Road   Cumberland,
Any State   34567   (165)555-5643**

Dear . . .

It is with great regret that I must decline my appointment as _____ at this time. It is an honor and a privilege to be considered for this position. Previous commitments and ever-demanding church responsibilities just make it impossible for me to take on anything else.

I subscribe to what Noel Coward once said: "Work is much more fun than fun." I'm having so much fun right now that if it gets any more fun . . . it'll stop being fun!

I'm sure you understand. Thank you again for thinking of me.

God's blessings upon your good work.

Gratefully,

Pastor Johnson

St. John's Community Church

5008 Wilkerson Avenue
Nashville, Any State 30662 (150)555-3057

Dear . . .

It is with great regret that I must decline your kind invitation to assume the (role/position) of _____. It is an honor to be considered for this important post in the denomination. If only there were more hours in the day—if only the daily demands of my parish weren't so relentless and all-consuming! Still, it is extremely difficult for me to pass up this wonderful opportunity.

In this instance, I have to believe that not only does God answer prayer, but sometimes the answer is an emphatic *no*. It seems apparent that my focus should remain here at St. John's Community Church. These are fine people here, and they deserve my full attention.

Thank you again for your kind and generous offer. I pray that you will understand my position. I trust that my present feelings will not close the door on future considerations.

Yours in Christ,

Pastor Johnson

A Letter to Write . . . and Then Shred!

Dear Pastor Across the Street . . .

Are you kiddin'? You want *me* to speak at one of your revival services! Sorry, I gotta beg off, pal. I have no glittery jewelry, I'm allergic to greasepaint, and I've never been able to cry on cue.

What are you running over there at your church—a game show? Is that stretch limo parked out in front yours, or is it a Sunday morning door prize? From what I hear, you're more a master of ceremonies than a minister of the gospel! Why does everybody in your congregation look so down and out, and you look so . . . so . . . *tailored?* I know I'm being judgmental and I shouldn't be. But just answer one thing—of the 1000-plus members in your church, how come you're the only one who looks so conspicuously out of place?

Your friend who drives the Nova.

Pastor Johnson

P.S. By the way, who does your hair?

CENTRAL BAPTIST CHURCH

Route 66   Longville,   Any State   98989
(111)555-3879

Dear . . .

Thank you for worshiping with us this past Sunday. If you are new to our community, welcome! If you are shopping around for a church home, please come again. There's something different and exciting happening nearly every week for persons of all ages.

You can be a "visitor" as long as you want. We won't pounce on you. We won't press, prod, or pry. We promise. We'll just be pleased as punch to have you among us, feeling comfortable and happy to be here.

In Christ,

Pastor Johnson

Emmanuel
Lutheran
Church

107 Brook Dr.

Bethay

Any State
45789

(199)555-6811

Dear . . .

I am happy to send you the enclosed information regarding membership at Emmanuel Lutheran
Church. This will give you an overview of our programs and special ministries, as well as specific
procedures for joining our vibrant church family.

As you already know, there is room at Emmanuel
for everyone. Regardless of background or previous church affiliation, you are warmly welcomed
here. Your request for membership information
indicates that you have thought long and hard
about your commitment of faith—and that perhaps
you have found what you've been looking for at
Emmanuel Lutheran Church.

Thank you for your request and for your interest. Most of all, however, we are grateful for your
presence among us. Please call me if you have any
concerns or questions.

In the meantime, there will be no pressure on
you to become a member. That decision is yours.
Take your time. We enjoy your being here.

Sincerely in Christ,

Pastor Johnson

Good Shepherd Community Church

968 Honeysuckle Road
Breezeville,   Any State   05050
Phone: (101)555-5467

Dear . . .

I am happy to send you the enclosed (information/packet) outlining the many programs and special ministries at Good Shepherd Community Church. Personally speaking, I appreciate your interest and welcome your involvement.

We are an active, talented bunch here at Good Shepherd. There are many niches to fill. Some are as traditional and long-standing as the church itself. Other niches are filled by people who come along and create them! Our ministries are malleable; that is, they are made to be unmade and to fit the ever-changing needs of our church and community.

Everybody fits here because there is room!

We welcome you here. Your degree of involvement is up to you. If you have any questions, please don't hesitate to call me.

May your faith give you direction. God's blessings upon you.

Pastor Johnson

Aldersgate United Methodist Church

23 West Crescent Blvd., Denton, Any State 77443
Phone: (173)555-4323

Dear . . .

I want to take this opportunity to welcome you into our church. I am grateful that you have chosen Aldersgate United Methodist Church to be your church home.

The church is an exciting place because of people like you who become part of it and, therefore, give it shape and texture. The church must never be static. It must always be changing and adapting to the personalities, the energies, the makeup of the people who are its very heart and soul.

I want you to use your energies here. Make this church what you want in a church. Find niches to fill. Or create them where they ought to be. This place is living matter. It is tissue and muscle. It is emotions and reason. Its parts are larger than the whole; for each of us is a sacred temple wherein God resides.

Because you are now a member of this church, this church is richer and more vibrant than it was! Thank you for helping to shape us anew!

God bless you.

Pastor Johnson

Christ Church

2010 Rural Hill Road
Standing Stone, Any State 12345
(155)555-1098

Dear . . .

One year ago you took the vows of membership and became part of our church family here at Christ Church. Your presence has meant a great deal to me. I have appreciated your participation and unique contributions to the life of this parish.

I trust you have found comfort and spiritual fulfillment here. I am glad you joined one year ago, and I thank God you have made Christ Church your church home.

Thanks for sharing you with us!

In Christ,

Pastor Johnson

TRINITY CHURCH

9005 WEST PARK AVENUE POUGHKEEPSIE, ANY STATE
00225
PHONE: (102)555-6744

Dear . . .

When the Bible was translated into English,
King Henry VIII made this comment in his speech
to Parliament on Christmas Eve, 1545:

> I am very sorry to know and hear how unreverent-
> ly that most precious jewel, the Word of God, is
> disputed, rhymed, sung and jangled in every ale-
> house and tavern, contrary to the true meaning
> and doctrine of the same.

King Henry was horrified at the notion that the
Scriptures could be so loosely bandied about, so
open to interpretation, so easily taken out of con-
text in order to satisfy one's own ends. Many of us
feel the same way today. That's why we welcome
the opportunity to probe for biblical truths
through thoughtful study and lively discussion.

You are invited to participate in this enlighten-
ing Bible study, _____. The class meets _____,
and there is room for you! Come with an open
mind, a willingness to share, and a serious desire
to learn.

Together in Christ,

Pastor Johnson

Calvary Church of Christ

One Windsor Commons   Green Hills,   Any State   23118   (178)555-9999

Dear . . .

On behalf of our church and the fellowship of churches in _____ (city/town), I would like to welcome you (and your family) to our community. I know how exhausting moving can be—how unsettling this kind of change is for everyone. Therefore, please accept this note as merely a hello, and as an invitation (with no obligation) to visit Calvary Church of Christ whenever you are settled, rested, and ready to meet a lot of wonderful folks.

In the meantime, please feel free to call me if you would just like to chat or ask directions to somewhere! Otherwise, I will certainly understand your need to have some time and space to adjust to your new surroundings.

Welcome to _____! May God give you strength and rest during this transition.

In Christ,

Richard Johnson

Faith Brethren Church

**776 Willowbrook Road   Cumberland,
Any State   34567 (165)555-5643**

Dear . . .

On behalf of the fellowship of Christian clergy in our community, I would like to extend a warm welcome to you (and your family)—and invite you to our home for coffee and cookies as soon as you feel up to it.

Moving is such an unsettling ordeal. For a while you'll be too busy (and too pooped) to care where the post office, the drugstore, and the running track are. But when you're ready, I'll be happy to give you directions or a personal tour.

Give me a call if you wish. Otherwise, I'll stay away—at least until you have the heavy stuff put away!

Welcome to _____. May God grant you (and your family) strength and rest during this transition.

In Christ,

Pastor Johnson

St. John's Community Church

5008 Wilkerson Avenue
Nashville, Any State 30662 (150)555-3057

Dear . . .

Congratulations on your new position in The United Methodist Church, and welcome to our (district, conference, area, jurisdiction). Your special talents will certainly enrich our ministry and encourage all of us to reach greater heights.

Please accept this as an open invitation to you (and your family) to visit St. John's whenever you can. I would consider it an honor to introduce you to the good people in this caring, loving parish.

May God grant you (and your family) renewed strength during this transition.

In Christ,

Pastor Johnson

A Letter to Write . . . and Then Shred!

Dear Henrietta Hawk . . .

Henrietta, I know you mean well, but would you please refrain from swooping down on first-time visitors like some harpy in heat! Gee whiz, I appreciate your evangelical zeal, but you're scaring them off even before we get the offering taken! I know you're the chairperson of Hospitality, but you will just have to do your gushing in moderation. Most folks don't care for having someone throw a cross-body block on them at the narthex door—or climb inside the backseat of their car after church! By the way, did they really want you to eat lunch with them at McDonald's—or, in the fervor of the moment, did you just sort of forget to get out of the car?

Henrietta dear, cool it! Cease and desist! In other words, just perch yourself in your pew and mind your own beeswax!

Imploringly yours,

Pastor Johnson

CENTRAL BAPTIST CHURCH

Route 66   Longville,   Any State   98989
(111)555-3879

Dear . . .

We hope our church mailings are reaching you properly and on time. We hope we're spelling your name correctly and that we have your address right on target. To ensure that we do, or to correct any blunders, please fill out the enclosed (card/form) and return it to the church office as soon as possible.

In addition to being accurate, we want our mailings to be as cost-effective as possible. By your helping us to update our church mailing list, we'll be able to eliminate any duplicate mailings and wrong addresses.

Thank you for your prompt assistance!

Pastor Johnson

**Emmanuel
Lutheran
Church**

107 Brook Dr.

Bethay

Any State
45789

(199)555-6811

Dear . . .

Occasionally it becomes necessary to update our membership records to make sure our information on our church members is accurate and complete. Since you (and your family) are new in our church, we would appreciate your completing the enclosed form and returning it to the church office at your earliest convenience.

Please write or print legibly. We want to be sure that all names (and spellings), addresses and dates are right on target.

Thank you for your promptness, thoroughness, and accuracy.

Pastor Johnson

Good Shepherd
Community Church

968 Honeysuckle Road
Breezeville,   Any State   05050
Phone: (101)555-5467

Dear . . .

Would you be so kind as to complete the enclosed form so that we can update (and/or) amend our church membership records. Occasionally it's a good idea to make sure we have all names and dates right—all i's dotted, t's crossed, and all i's before e's except for the exceptions!

Please write or print legibly, fill out the form completely, and then return it to the church office at your earliest convenience. Your promptness, thoroughness, and accuracy will be appreciated.

Thanks!

Pastor Johnson

Dear . . .

Often we pastors get raked over the coals for prying, prodding, arm-twisting, even hounding. Well, I hope this brief note is accepted in the spirit in which it is intended—as merely an inquiry to find out if (you/you folks) are all right.

It seems as though I haven't seen you in church for quite a while. If you're on an extended Caribbean cruise, I'm a little green (with envy). If you've found another church home, I'm a little blue (but I wish you well just the same).

However, if you're finding a lot of diversions on Sunday morning and keep having good intentions of returning to your pew here at Aldersgate United Methodist Church, then let me just say I miss you and hope to see you back soon.

Whatever the reason for your extended absence, give me a call to let me know you're O.K. Do it right now. That would make my day.

Please call or drop me a line. Thanks!

Yours in Christ,

Pastor Johnson

Christo Church

2010 Rural Hill Road
Standing Stone, Any State 12345
(155)555-1098

Dear . . .

Church membership rolls, like shrubs and long letters, occasionally need pruning. And although we're not eager to remove your name from our membership roll at Christ Church, your long absence indicates that you may be attending elsewhere.

Soon it will be our unhappy task to do just that—remove your name from our membership roll unless we hear from you no later than _____ (date).

If you have found another church home, we certainly want to wish you well. I'm sure you can understand our need to keep our records as current as possible.

Thank you for your help. God's blessings on you (and your family).

Pastor Johnson

TRINITY CHURCH

9005 WEST PARK AVENUE   POUGHKEEPSIE, ANY STATE
00225
PHONE: (102)555-6744

Dear . . .

It is with great pleasure and some sadness that I send you this Transfer of Membership Letter on behalf of _____.

You and your church are the benefactors of a fine (Christian/Christian family). (He/she/they) (has/have) been part of our parish family for _____ years and (has/have) served as a great source of energy and inspiration. We will miss (him/her/them). (He/she/they) (leaves/leave) behind a legacy of love freely shared.

I entreat you to cultivate (his/her/their) many talents. (His/her/their) presence will enrich your life and the lives of those you serve. My prayers go with (him/her/them) and with you.

May you forge a beautiful partnership for the glory of our Lord and Savior, Jesus Christ!

May God bless your ministry.

Pastor Johnson

Calvary Church of Christ

Calvary Church of Christ
Calvary Church of Christ

One Windsor Commons   Green Hills,   Any State   23118   (178)555-9999

Dear . . .

On behalf of all your old friends at Calvary Church of Christ, I would like to extend warm greetings to you (and your family) and let you know that we miss you a bunch!

It should be of some comfort to you to know that your spirit and vitality remain. And although (you/you folks) left a considerable void (not easily filled), we are doing our best to carry on your fine tradition of jumping in with both feet and getting things done!

We hope and pray that you are getting settled. We know it won't take you long to get into the thick of things at your new church. Perhaps you've already taken the plunge. If so, then your new friends must realize by now that God has richly blessed them.

Best wishes to you. We love you and miss you. Please come back for a visit whenever you can.

Fondly,

Richard Johnson

A Letter to Write . . . and Then Shred!

Dear Ever-Faithful . . .

We missed you this past Easter Sunday. Hope to see you next year.

In anticipation,

Pastor Johnson

P.S. I'll bet your kids have grown!

Faith Brethren Church

**776 Willowbrook Road   Cumberland,
Any State   34567 (165)555-5643**

Dear . . .

If it's true that "absence makes the heart grow fonder," then there must be a lot of folks out there who dearly love our church! That's why we want to advertise in _____ (name of newspaper).

Enclosed is a rough layout of our ad. As per our discussion on the phone, we would like to run the ad _____ (dates/frequency) at a total cost of $_____. We understand that you will bill us at the church address above. Please direct your billing to the attention of _____.

If you have any questions about the wording or design of the ad, please give me a call at my office, _____ (phone #). When it is typeset and ready to go, I would appreciate the opportunity of giving it one last look before you go to press.

Thank you for your help and cooperation.

Sincerely,

Pastor Johnson

St. John's Community Church

5008 Wilkerson Avenue
Nashville, Any State 30662 (150)555-3057

Dear . . .

They say that any publicity is good publicity, but in the case of your recent story about _____, nothing could be farther from the truth. To our chagrin, it contains erroneous information that both misleads and does a disservice to the fine people and programs at St. John's Community Church.

Allow me to point out the specific inaccuracies, after which I trust your newspaper will respond in an appropriate and professional manner—namely with a printed apology and a revised story.

(details)

Sincerely,

Pastor Johnson

CENTRAL BAPTIST CHURCH
Route 66   Longville,   Any State   98989
(111)555-3879

Dear . . .

We folks in the religious community often seem reluctant to pat ourselves on the back or to sing our own praises, even when we should. We talk about sharing the "Good News," but we often don't share our own good news. Sometimes we don't even look like we're having any fun. No wonder people think we're a gloomy bunch!

Well, so much for gloom and doom. Forget about that Christian austerity. We have something to shout about at Central Baptist Church, and we want to share it with everyone within your newspaper's reach! It portrays the Christian life in a positive, upbeat manner. That's why I am proud to be the one to share our good news with you!

(details)

We will be most grateful for your interest in developing this story for your fine newspaper. Please call me for additional information. Should I not hear from you within the week, I will be happy to call your office.

Thank you. May your every day be good news!

Sincerely,

Pastor Johnson

Emmanuel Lutheran Church

107 Brook Dr.

Bethay

Any State
45789

(199)555-6811

Dear . . .

On behalf of all of us at Emmanuel Lutheran Church, I would like to thank you and your staff for the positive support you have provided us over the year(s).

You have done for us what our limited funds and resources could never do—you have carried our story of Christian faith and good works into countless homes throughout the area. Because of that, we have welcomed many new faces into our church family. You deserve much of the credit for our church's renewed growth and expanding ministries.

Thank you for your kindness and your professionalism. May God continue to bless your fine work in the community.

Gratefully yours,

Pastor Johnson

Good Shepherd Community Church

968 Honeysuckle Road
Breezeville, Any State   05050
Phone: (101)555-5467

Dear . . .

On behalf of all of us at Good Shepherd Community Church, I would like to thank you and your staff for the skillful reporting of the story about _____. Your coverage was generous and first-rate.

A story like this, carried into the countless homes throughout the area, not only is wonderful publicity for Good Shepherd, but it also raises everyone's awareness of Christianity with its sleeves rolled up! You deserve much of the credit for a revival of enthusiasm and effort here at Good Shepherd Community Church.

Thank you for your story. May God continue to bless your fine work in the community.

Gratefully yours,

Pastor Johnson

A Letter to Write . . . and Then Shred!

Dear Reporter (?) . . .

If I were your editor, I'd do you a favor and red pencil your career as a journalist! Where in the blue blazes did you get your information for the story about our church? It's obvious that your research didn't include fact-finding. It's also clear that your regard for truth and accuracy will open important doors for you professionally—selling used cars!

Would you please try it again and get it right! I have some pretty hot-under-the-collar parishioners who have just about lost their religion—and who would like to write an article of their own—YOUR OBITUARY!

Your Riled Reverend,

Pastor Johnson

Letters to Vendors

Dear . . .

Because of your fine reputation as a business (man/woman) and building contractor, the administrative board and trustees of the Aldersgate United Methodist Church, located at _____, have authorized me to give you the opportunity to bid on the construction of our new education wing.

Let me assure you at the outset that we are not interested only in the cost. Although dollars are a primary concern, we are just as interested in quality of work, adherence to a reasonable timetable, professional personnel (including all subcontractors), access to the contractor and building superintendent in case of questions or concerns, and a commitment to following through on all promises and agreements to our satisfaction.

Please call my office as soon as possible so that we can schedule a meeting to go over details and answer any questions. Preliminary plans for the annex have been drawn up and will be available to you at that time.

I might add at this early juncture that we feel confident that financing for this venture will be secured with reasonable dispatch.

I look forward to hearing from you quite soon so that we can discuss the particulars and begin the bidding process. Incidentally, when you submit your bid, we will also appreciate your furnishing us with three client references representing recently completed projects.

Thank you.

Sincerely,

Pastor Johnson

Christt Church

2010 Rural Hill Road
Standing Stone, Any State 12345
(155)555-1098

Dear . . .

The administrative board and trustees of Christ Church, located at _____, have authorized me to write and request a price quote from your company.

We are shopping for a new _____ for use in our church, and we are hoping to make a purchase by no later than _____ (date). Enclosed is a detailed description with specifications of _____ (item) to assist you in giving us as accurate a quote as possible.

Please feel free to call me if you have any questions regarding our request. We would appreciate your sending us a written itemized quote so that we can have it in hand for committee consideration and discussion.

Thank you for your good service and prompt response.

Sincerely,

Pastor Johnson

A Letter to Write . . . and Then Shred!

Dear Phony . . . er . . . Photocopier Company . . .

If I could I'd load your photocopier into my car and dump it at your front door! That's the very least I could do, since you crooks obviously *unloaded it on us!*

Maybe we should have a funeral for it and give it a proper burial. No, on second thought, that would be a waste of dirt!

Look, you lunkheads, if you can't repair our copy machine so that it works for more than a week at a time, then give us our money back. I'd get better, faster, and more consistent copy service from a stooped-back monk and a quill pen!

Pastor Johnson

P.S.   ! The foregoing sentence in this postscript demonstrates the copy clarity of your machine—on the "darker" setting!

pc: To no one! How could we?

TRINITY CHURCH

9005 WEST PARK AVENUE   POUGHKEEPSIE, ANY STATE
00225
PHONE: (102)555-6744

Dear Church Member . . .

"Stewardship" isn't an idea that some money-minded theologian conjured up. Nor is it a fancy term for money-grubbing con artists who are more at home on a stage than in a pulpit.

Although "stewardship" often gets a bum rap because of our own snap judgments and short-sightedness, it is a concept firmly grounded in scripture. Stewardship is an attitude of serving. The Christian steward worships, studies, gives, and loves. He or she does so willingly and freely. And he or she is grateful to God for the privilege.

Stewardship is our response to God's grace. In I Corinthians 9:17, Paul writes, "For if I do this of my own will, I have a reward, but if not of my own will, I am entrusted with a commission." And in Ephesians 3:2, he says, "For surely you have already heard of the commission of God's grace that was given me for you." And in verse 7, he goes on to say, "Of this gospel I have become a servant according to the gift of God's grace that was given me by the working of his power."

I encourage all of us to change our perspective on the meaning of stewardship. Stewardship is not our effort—through our time, talents, and money—to create a relationship with God. It is a *response* to God—with our time, talents, and money—because of our personal relationship with him *that already exists* through his son, Jesus Christ! We practice good stewardship not to receive gratitude, but to show gratitude for that special relationship that is yours and mine—*no strings attached.*

Jesus said, "Follow me." Stewardship, my dear friends, is the fulfillment of that incredible offer!

In Christ,

Pastor Johnson

Calvary Church of Christ

One Windsor Commons   Green Hills,   Any State   23118   (178)555-9999

Dear Church Member . . .

I like what Thomas L. Are writes in his book, *My Gospel of Stewardship*. He describes stewardship as a "Life-Style Plan." Stewardship is more than an act that is performed. It is a way of life.

Stewardship involves laying a solid foundation upon which to build a Christian life. That foundation includes: *Worship*—getting to know God and yourself; *Study*—improving your mind in order to magnify the gifts God has given to you; *Service* (not duty, but service)—allowing yourself to be used for the good of others and for the glory of God; *Giving*—sharing your resources freely, since all that you *have* and all that you *are* have been given to you by God; *Reconciliation*—creating, healing, or enhancing loving relationships with others in order to break down the barriers that separate us. Wow!

I challenge each of you to expand your perception of Christian stewardship. Think of it as more than a pledge envelope or a weekly commitment or holding an office in the church. Think of stewardship as a deeper, more holistic way of Christian living that will gradually lead to greater "selfless discovery"!

Dear God, may we open our eyes to see—our hearts to feel—and our minds to understand the limitless potential of living as true Christian stewards.

In Christ,

Richard Johnson

Faith Brethren Church

**776 Willowbrook Road   Cumberland,
Any State   34567 (165)555-5643**

Dear Church Member . . .

I think it's worthwhile to include a reminder
every once in a while about what Christian stewardship really entails. This is especially necessary
as we are about to embark on our annual church
pledge campaign. Although this important
endeavor falls under the stewardship umbrella,
that same umbrella encompasses more than just
dollars and cents.

Being a good steward means taking care of our
church in every way. All of us need to be caretakers of our building and facilities. Yes, we pay our
church custodians to help keep our church property clean and functional. But Christ commissions
each of us to pitch in willingly and freely, with our
minds and our muscle, to help preserve our house
of worship.

We are also required, as stewards of Christ's
Church, to give of our skills and talents. For even
if we had no physical structure called a church,
our faith, coupled with our talents and abilities,
would make us no less a temple of worship. When
the Christian steward leads, directs, comforts,
teaches, sings, plans, coordinates, organizes,
cooks, decorates, and *loves doing it*—then the
church becomes a powerful force of solidarity and
service.

The church needs your dollars and cents. However, stewardship that does not go beyond the

pocketbook is shallow. Monetarily, we are all on different planes. Some are better off than others. When it comes to talents and abilities, however, all of us are millionaires!

Come on! Let's share the wealth!

In Christ's service,

Pastor Johnson

St. John's Community Church

5008 Wilkerson Avenue
Nashville, Any State 30662 (150)555-3057

Dear . . .

It is our pleasure and privilege at St. John's Community Church to be able to make our facilities available not only to church groups, but also to outside organizations. We are glad that we can provide space for worthwhile programs and activities. Part of our mission as Christian stewards is to make the best use of our space and resources. This is Christ's Church, after all. And we are the caretakers.

Enclosed is a copy of our rules and regulations for the care and use of the church facilities as determined by the St. John's Community Church administrative board and trustees. These policies have been established to ensure that the church property is maintained in the best possible manner so that everyone can use and enjoy what Christ has entrusted to us.

We welcome you at St. John's Community Church. Thank you for your cooperation.

In Christ's service,

Pastor Johnson

CENTRAL BAPTIST CHURCH

Route 66   Longville,   Any State   98989
(111)555-3879

Dear . . .

Someone once said, "The trouble with being poor is that it takes up all your time." How true. When a person must concern himself or herself with daily survival, self-sufficiency is an impossibility.

I would like to ask each of you to give generously to our Food for the Poor program. I would also like to remind you that the opposite of poverty is not wealth, but *adequacy*. Adequacy—simply having enough of the essentials to live.

Our donations of food will not solve the hunger problem in our community. But we can alleviate the misery that is such a constant companion to so many. We may even make it possible for one person to rise above *adequacy* and achieve some measure of independence. When that happens, a person has time to dream!

In his speech to the World Food Congress in 1963, John Kennedy said, "The war against hunger is truly mankind's war of liberation." This is one war worth the fight!

Please give generously. Bring your food donations to the church _____ (specifics).

Thank you. God's blessings upon each of you.

Pastor Johnson

Dear . . .

    Someone in our church family urgently needs our help in the form of a cash or food donation. It really isn't important who this person is. Our concern ought to be that the need exists, and that we are blessed to be in a position to help.

    As your pastor and as the shepherd of this caring congregation, I am asking that you give generously. Give as you have received.

    II Corinthians 9:7 reminds us: "Each of you must give as you have made up your mind, not reluctantly or under compulsion, for God loves a cheerful giver."

    If you will help, here's how to go about it. (Explain logistics of contributing cash and/or food.)

    Thank you for your help. May God continue to bless you and your loved ones.

In Christ,

Pastor Johnson

Emmanuel Lutheran Church

107 Brook Dr.

Bethay

Any State
45789

(199)555-6811

Good Shepherd Community Church

968 Honeysuckle Road
Breezeville, Any State 05050
Phone: (101)555-5467

Dear . . .

Do you have an extra room or spare bed in your home? Would you like to put it to good use and, at the same time, help someone in our church family? Your time and expense will be minimal—the impact of your goodwill immeasurable!

Recently a member of our church suffered a misfortune that could happen to any of us. Without naming names or going into detail, let me assure you that the need for housing is both urgent and temporary.

If you have space available in your own home, or if you know of someone who does, please call me immediately for a confidential chat. Your show of interest in no way obligates you to additional service. However, I would welcome the opportunity to meet with you to discuss the possibilities.

All inquiries will be confidential. Please let me hear from you soon.

"All our doings without charity are nothing worth" *(The Book of Common Prayer)*.

Thank you.

In Christ's service,

Pastor Johnson

Dear . . .

Perhaps a letter shouldn't be necessary in asking for help for the _____ family. After all, we are a caring, sharing church. When help is needed in any form, we are ready and eager to do our part.

However, all of us are busy people—often so caught up in the day-to-day demands of living that we forget the moment-by-moment distress of others. I am writing this brief letter, therefore, as a friendly but urgent reminder that the _____ family needs our help in order to get through the hours, days, and weeks ahead.

How fragile and dear life is! How suddenly our peace and comfort can be shattered, often through no fault of our own. How fortunate most of us are that we are seldom tested to such an extent!

As you reflect on your many blessings, won't you likewise think of the ways in which you can help the _____s? Whether you give food, clothes, or money, your gifts will help them get back on their feet so that they can regain their self-sufficiency.

Here's how you can give. (Explain details of how, when, and where.)

Remember, there, but for the grace of God, go you and I.

Thank you. God bless you.

Pastor Johnson

Christ Church

2010 Rural Hill Road
Standing Stone, Any State 12345
(155)555-1098

Dear . . .

"For I was hungry and you gave me food, I was thirsty and you gave me something to drink, I was a stranger and you welcomed me" (Matthew 25:35).

Most of you probably know by now about the tragedy that has struck the _____ family in our community. As part of our Christian outreach in _____ (town, city), I am appealing to all members of Christ Church for your help and support.

The _____ family needs your prayers, first and foremost. They also need food and clothes or the funds to purchase those things. The need is urgent and great. Our willingness to help meet this need ought to equal the challenge!

If you have a contribution, here's what you should do. (Explain details of how, when, and where.)

In terms of living our Christianity, it's time to roll up our sleeves and get to work! Please help.

Thank you. God bless you.

Pastor Johnson

TRINITY CHURCH

9005 WEST PARK AVENUE   POUGHKEEPSIE, ANY STATE
00225
PHONE: (102)555-6744

Dear . . .

"Evangelical outreach." It's a real mouthful. For many, it's also hard to swallow.

"Evangelical outreach." The term conjures up knocking on doors, distributing tracts on street corners, and twisting arms. It is synonymous with putting the squeeze on someone, applying enough pressure until he or she finally succumbs from sheer exhaustion.

"Evangelical outreach" at Trinity Church is none of the above. When you support "evangelical outreach" programs through your giving, you're contributing to such things as church advertising and promotion, the church newsletter, the church directory, as well as our participation in worthwhile community events.

The church exists primarily for those who don't go near it. Our task as "outreachers" is not to see how many bodies we can drag into our fold. Instead, "evangelical outreach" challenges us to take our church beyond its doors, into the light of day and the dark of night—to share our faith with a hostile but hungry world by *living our faith,* not peddling it.

I invite you to support the "evangelical outreach" programs here at Trinity Church through your giving. Here the Good News is shared with skill and sensitivity—and with the help of a few of your dollars. Please give.

Thank you. May God grant you abundant blessings.

Pastor Johnson

Calvary Church of Christ

One Windsor Commons   Green Hills,   Any State   23118   (178)555-9999

Dear . . .

As we launch our campaign to support church missions, let me remind you that much of our mission work takes place right here in the United States. Some of it happens right here in our own city!

It's funny how we always equate Christian missions with foreign lands and peoples. Although it's true that much of our church mission work is carried to the four corners of the earth, a great many missionaries in our denomination never leave our shores. And many of your mission dollars stay right here to support Christ's work in our streets, shelters, and schools.

I encourage you to support our church missions program. There is much to be done right here at home. Please give generously.

If you want to know more about our mission work here in the United States, please call _____.

Thank you. God's blessings upon you.

Richard Johnson

Faith Brethren Church

**776 Willowbrook Road   Cumberland,
Any State   34567 (165)555-5643**

Dear . . .

John Wesley said, "The world is my parish."
With that in mind, allow me to share a thought or
two with you regarding our financial support of
mission work in the far corners of nearly every
nation on earth.

When it comes to giving to mission work, many
of us would rather take care of only ourselves. It is
difficult to support foreign mission work that is far
away and invisible, familiar to us only through
denominational brochures and reports. We would
rather see our mission giving firsthand, here at
home, across town, or down the street. Under-
standably, we believe in Christian missions when
we can *see* it in action.

However, let me offer some food for thought.
Christian charity ought not to have borders or
boundaries. If we allow our church missions support to become too parochial, then we are attach-
ing conditions to Christian outreach—which, by its
very definition, must be offered unconditionally.
Otherwise, the work of Christian missions becomes a selfish rather than selfless undertaking.

I encourage you to support Christian mission
work both here at home and abroad. I implore you to
give out of faith that your gift will be used to further
Christ's word and work. Foreign mission work cannot survive without collective help from you and me.

Please give to our foreign missions program.
Thank you.

In Christ's service,

Pastor Johnson

St. John's Community Church

5008 Wilkerson Avenue
Nashville, Any State 30662 (150)555-3057

Dear . . .

Here at St. John's we shall one day realize what is today still a dream. And that dream is to have a new addition to our _____ (sanctuary, education building, etc.).

We all agree that an expansion program is urgently needed here at St. John's. We are a continually growing church, and we must be prepared to meet the needs of a growing and diverse community. Our proposed new addition will give us the room to do more and do it better.

As you prepare to make your pledge to St. John's, I encourage you to earmark a portion for the church Building Fund. Without your financial support, our dream will remain just that—a dream. Dreams are wonderful, but they're not real. Let's make our dream a reality!

In your giving, please remember to support our church Building Fund.

Thank you. God bless you.

Pastor Johnson

CENTRAL BAPTIST CHURCH

Route 66   Longville,   Any State   98989
(111)555-3879

Dear . . .

Sometimes it's better to put some things behind us and get on with something else. A debt is like that. In our case, I'm referring to our mortgage debt here at Central Baptist Church.

Wouldn't it be nice to retire our debt early and keep all that interest for other things? Let's do it! If we all dig a little deeper throughout the next several weeks—perhaps an additional $_____ per giving unit—we'll be able to pay off our debt by _____. If we do that, we'll save approximately $_____.

Let's each make this a personal pledge. Increase your weekly giving by just $_____ for the next _____ (weeks, months), and we'll be able to put the whole thing behind us by _____! What a wonderful feeling that would be!

Let's do it!

If anyone would like to examine the figures close up, please feel free to call _____.

Thank you.

In Christ,

Pastor Johnson

Emmanuel Lutheran Church

107 Brook Dr.

Bethay

Any State
45789

(199)555-6811

Dear . . .

The old deacon was fond of always saying, "I'm not making much progress, but I'm well established." This was his stock excuse for his narrow-mindedness.

One day, after a spring thaw, the deacon climbed into his pickup truck to go into town. On his way, he got stuck in mud. Minutes later, a fellow church member drove up, stopped, and quipped, "Well, you're not making much progress, but you're well established!"

As you read this year-end report—this "state of Emmanuel Lutheran Church address"—I think you'll agree that not only are we a well-established church, but we have made great strides as a growing, caring congregation. As your pastor, I am proud of where we've been and where we're going. We have not stood still, satisfied with our accomplishments. Yes, we have done good things this past year for the glory of the Kingdom, but even greater challenges lie ahead.

God commands us to grow. GROW. To grow in our understanding of *God*—in our *R*elationships with one another—in the development of *O*urselves—and in the understanding of our *W*orld. GROW.

As we look back over this past year and look ahead at the infinite possibilities yet unrealized, let us use GROW as a guidepost to keep us on a path of wisdom and spiritual maturity.

Thanks be to God for a growing church—past, present, and future.

In Christ,

Pastor Johnson

Good Shepherd Community Church

968 Honeysuckle Road
Breezeville, Any State 05050
Phone: (101)555-5467

Dear . . .

On behalf of Good Shepherd Community Church, our administrative board, and our task force on _____, I am submitting a complete, formal request for grant funds. It is my earnest hope that we have presented this proposal in the proper fashion. If, for any reason, additional information or a change in format is necessary, we will be happy to respond accordingly and re-submit our application.

In the enclosed packet, you will find the following:

1. Title page (including abstract; i.e., statement of what problem our research will address, and what it attempts to accomplish)
2. Table of contents
3. Amplified abstract (i.e., detailed statement of the problem and statement of the solution)
4. Time schedule
5. Budget
6. Addenda

In our grant proposal, we will answer the following questions in order for you to make an objective and fair evaluation:

—What do we want to do?
—Why do we want to do it?
—How are we going to do it?
—Who is going to do it?
—Where are we going to do it?
—How long will it take?

—How much will it cost?
—What significant contribution will our research make to the specific field of _____?

We are not experts when it comes to applying for a grant. However, our intent is sincere, and our commitment to this important work is unwavering. It is our belief that the church and its auxiliary agencies can and should be expanding our knowledge of the world through examination, discovery, and enlightenment.

We have thought through this research process. We are confident that the work we propose will be the work produced. It is certainly our hope to build a track record that will increase our chances to procure support and funding for future projects.

Thank you for the opportunity and for your assistance. We will eagerly await your reply.

Sincerely,

Pastor Johnson

Note: *This letter will vary according to the type of funding requested and the funding agency. In some cases, agencies require and furnish standardized forms.*

A Letter to Write . . . and Then Shred!

Dear Busy, Busy, Busy Member . . .

When the cookies are brought out for coffee hour, you're always first in line to grab a handful. But you're never in line when it comes to providing them. When the annual church dinner is announced, you're invariably among the first to jump up and yell, "I'll help . . . !" But you never finish your sentence. "I'll help . . . *to eat!*" (I'm curious, do you even know how a folding chair works?) When a volunteer is needed, you can reel off names faster than anyone!

You know, as far as enjoying all the benefits of our faith and fellowship here at Church of the Cross, you really know how to work up a sweat. One might even say that as a Christian steward, you're a real drip!

As always,

Pastor Johnson

Your faithful servant

TRINITY CHURCH

Stewardship/Finance Campaign Schedule

- 4 to 5 weeks prior to Pledge Sunday . . . introductory letter from pastor
- 4th Sunday before . . . bulletin insert #1
- 3rd Sunday before . . . bulletin insert #2
- Approximately two weeks before . . . second letter from pastor, with pledge card, sent between the 2nd and 3rd Sundays of the campaign
- 2nd Sunday before . . . bulletin insert #3
- Sunday before . . . bulletin insert #4

This stewardship/finance campaign can be adapted to any time of the year. Some word changes may be in order, depending on the season.

Obviously some of the language and terminology used in the initial letter, bulletin inserts, and second letter will need to be revised, depending on the denomination and the programs in any given congregation.

TRINITY CHURCH

9005 WEST PARK AVENUE   POUGHKEEPSIE, ANY STATE
00225
PHONE: (102)555-6744

There are three kinds of giving: grudge giving, duty giving, and thanksgiving. Grudge giving says, "I hate to," duty giving says, "I ought to," and thanksgiving says, *"I want to."* The first comes from constraint, the second from a sense of obligation, the third from a full heart.

—*Robert Rodenmayer*

Dear Friend of Trinity Church . . .

It is time once again for each of us to renew our financial commitment to Trinity Church for _____ (year). The church will receive your pledge on Sunday, _____ (date).

This year, let us each make an earnest effort to increase our pledge—not grudgingly, nor out of a sense of obligation—but from a full heart. In other words, let your financial covenant with Trinity Church emerge from a true sense of thanksgiving for what this church means to you and for how this fellowship of Christian friends has enriched your life.

You know, nothing much is conveyed through grudge giving, the feeling of paying your dues, since "the gift without the giver is bare." There may be something a bit more admirable in duty giving, but there's no joy or enthusiasm in duty giving. Thanksgiving, however, opens the heart and the heart suddenly fills with thanksgiving! It's true and it's wonderful. Giving out of thanks fills the heart with thanksgiving!

Therefore, if we were to coin a slogan for this year's financial pledge campaign, it might be, "Give out of thanksgiving—with a full heart!"

GIVE OUT OF THANKSGIVING—WITH A FULL HEART!

Each of us must ask himself or herself an important question: What has Trinity Church meant to me that fills my heart with thanksgiving? Is there truly any one of us whose life has not been touched in some way by this vibrant, supportive church family? Think for a moment . . .

—Does your child attend Sunday school?
—Has your child attended Vacation Church School?
—Does the pastor's sermon provide nourishment for your spirit?
—Do you enjoy the choir cantatas and other special music programs?
—Do you enjoy our bell choir? Our children's choir?
—Do you appreciate seeing our youngsters participate as acolytes, presiders, readers, and greeters?
—Do you enjoy the special seasonal programs, the pageants, musicals, and so on?
—Have you enjoyed the numerous church outings throughout the year?
—Does it make you feel good just to rub shoulders with the terrific and talented people in our congregation?

Or perhaps what fills your heart most about Trinity Church is best described by words from "Blest Be the Tie That Binds":

> We share each other's woes,
> our mutual burdens bear;
> and often for each other flows
> the sympathizing tear.

P. 3

As each of you contemplates and prays about your financial commitment to Trinity Church, think of the comfort you feel (or have felt) in just knowing that this community of believers is here ready always to lend you a hand—to offer you a shoulder, to help share your burden, to celebrate your triumphs, to wipe away your tears, to love you no matter what.

GIVE OUT OF THANKSGIVING—WITH A FULL HEART!

Here's how . . .

1. *Pledge generously.* Increase your pledge if you can. Someone once said that you needn't give until it hurts . . . you ought to give until it feels good!
2. *Make sure you meet your pledge.* Whether you are able to increase your pledge or not, please follow through on your commitment.
3. *Pray about your pledge.* Think about what Trinity Church means to you. Then give out of thanksgiving—with a full heart! "Freely ye have received, freely give" (Matthew 10:8 KJV).

Think about Trinity Church. Pray for Trinity Church. Pray about your financial commitment to Trinity Church. Reflect on what this church means and has meant to you and your family. Then give out of thanksgiving—with a full heart!

May God bless you as you prepare to make your financial covenant with Trinity Church for the new year.

Thank you.

Pastor Johnson

TRINITY CHURCH

Pledge Sunday is _____ (date).

GIVE OUT OF THANKSGIVING—WITH A FULL HEART!

Before our Father's throne
we pour our ardent prayers;
our fears, our hopes, our aims are one,
our comforts and our cares.

We share each other's woes,
our mutual burdens bear;
and often for each other flows
the sympathizing tear.

—From "Blest Be the Tie That Binds"

As each of you prays about your financial commitment to Trinity Church, think of the comfort you feel in just knowing that this church is here, ready always to lend you a hand—to offer you a shoulder, to help share your burden, to celebrate your triumphs, to wipe away your tears, to love and support you no matter what.

As you prepare to make your pledge for _____ (year), do so in the spirit of thanksgiving—with a full heart!

TRINITY CHURCH

Pledge Sunday is _____ (date).

GIVE OUT OF THANKSGIVING—WITH A FULL HEART!

Did you know . . .

—that our monthly mortgage is _____?

—that to cover our mortgage payments, the church budget was increased by $ _____ a year?

—that during the months of _____, we fell short on our mortgage payments by a total of $_____?

—that already church staff salaries have been frozen or cut?

—that if our monthly giving continues to fall short, we will slowly deplete what cash reserves we have?

—that, as a result, we will begin the new year with virtually no cash reserves at all?

—that some of our last pledges have gone unfulfilled?

We need your help. We need your financial commitment to Trinity Church. We need you to *make it* and to *keep it*. As you prepare to make your financial covenant with Trinity Church for _____ (year), do so in the spirit of thanksgiving—with a full heart!

TRINITY CHURCH

9005 WEST PARK AVENUE   POUGHKEEPSIE, ANY STATE
00225
PHONE: (102)555-6744

Dear Friend of Trinity Church,

Thank you in advance for your financial pledge to Trinity Church that you will make on Sunday _____ (date). I know that your commitment will be made after much thought and prayer.

I know that you will give what you can . . . out of thanksgiving—with a full heart.

If, however, you have not come to a decision about your _____ (year) pledge, I encourage you to reread the first stewardship letter you received a couple of weeks ago. (If you did not receive one, please call the church office immediately.) I also urge you to go back and reread the bulletin inserts you have received the past two Sundays—and to make sure you read the inserts coming up the following two Sundays. The letter and the inserts will refresh your memory as to the real dollars and cents needs of our church in order to meet our mortgage and ministry responsibilities.

Certainly no one wants to see one commitment shortchanged in order to fulfill another. To be a whole church, we need to remain wholly committed and wholly alive. The building blocks of our many programs are just as vital as the blocks of our building. Both structures need our continued support through our prayers, service, and gifts.

This pledge campaign, quite obviously, underscores our giving power in real dollars and cents. Quite simply, the church needs money to operate. It is never easy to ask for money. But the easiest way to do it when it must be done . . . is to state the facts, present the needs, and ask each of you to respond according to your own willingness and ability.

P. 2

Your pledge is a very private decision. So no matter what your decision—whether you are able to increase your pledge, to maintain your present pledge amount, or whether you choose not to pledge at all—thank you for giving this matter serious and prayerful consideration. **Give out of a sense of thanksgiving—with a full heart!** Thank you.

Wishing you God's blessings,

Pastor Johnson

P.S. If you will not be attending the worship service on Pledge Sunday, Sunday, _____ (date), you may deliver or mail your Pledge Card to the church office.

TRINITY CHURCH

Pledge Sunday is _____ (date).

GIVE OUT OF THANKSGIVING—WITH A FULL HEART!

There are three kinds of giving: grudge giving, duty giving, and thanksgiving. Grudge giving says, "I hate to," duty giving says, "I ought to," and thanksgiving says, *"I want to."* The first comes from constraint, the second from a sense of obligation, the third from a full heart.

—*Robert Rodenmayer*

Here's what you can do on Sunday, _____ (date):

1. *Pledge generously.* Increase your pledge if you can. Someone once said that you needn't give until it hurts—you ought to give until it feels good.
2. *Make a pledge to fulfill your pledge.* Whether you are able to increase your pledge or not, please follow through on your commitment.
3. *Pray about your pledge.* Think about what Trinity Church means to you. Then give out of thanksgiving—with a full heart! "Freely ye have received, freely give" (Matthew 10:8 KJV).

As you prepare to make your pledge for _____ (year), do so in the spirit of thanksgiving—with a full heart!

TRINITY CHURCH

Pledge Sunday is next Sunday.

GIVE OUT OF THANKSGIVING—WITH A FULL HEART!

A Giving Guideline For You . . .

There are 120 "giving units" (individuals and families) in our congregation. Our annual operating budget is approximately $140,000. If you divide $140,000 by 120, you have $1167.00. If you divide that amount by 52 (weeks a year), the result is $22.44.

If each "giving unit" represented $22.44 a week to our church, our financial commitments to both our mortgage and our ministries would be met.

Please don't panic. The above figures are only guidelines to help you measure your giving ability. For some of you, $22.44 a week is an impossibility. For others of you, however, that weekly amount may be entirely realistic. Still others may be able to exceed that weekly amount.

Give what you can in a spirit of thanksgiving—with a full heart!

Thank you. May God bless you as you prepare to make your financial covenant for the new year.

A Letter to Write . . . and Then Shred!

Dear Board President,

Were you born *late?* Have you ever been on time for anything in your life? You're always complaining that no one comes to board meetings, that they're apathetic and uncaring. That ain't it, pal. They're just tired of breaking their necks to get here for a 7:30 board meeting, when they have to twiddle their thumbs waiting for you to show up at 7:45! I don't blame them. I wouldn't come to your meetings either if I didn't have to. But since I'm the pastor, I feel this nagging obligation. In other words, I get paid to suffer fools. Believe me, as far as I'm concerned, your lack of punctuality (not to mention organization) is in direct proportion to the lack of participation by your fellow parishioners.

You're supposed to be a leader in the church. *So lead!*

Impatiently yours,

Pastor Johnson

Service Pledge Campaign Schedule

- 5 to 6 weeks prior to Service Pledge Sunday . . . introductory letter from pastor

- 4th Sunday before . . . bulletin insert #1

- 3rd Sunday before . . . bulletin insert #2

- 3rd Sunday before . . . letter to member, with Service Pledge packet

- 2nd Sunday before . . . bulletin insert #3

- Sunday before . . . bulletin insert #4

This campaign is based on Service Pledge Sunday being whatever is regarded as Christmas Sunday in any given year. However, this campaign could be adapted to any time of the year with just a few word changes. Obviously, in order for this campaign to be a success, it requires a great deal of advance planning by members of the church council and the pastor—as well as thorough follow-up and evaluation by the same people at the end of the year. Once people have filled out their Service Pledges and have made a commitment for the new year, the real work of the pastor and church council members has just begun. And so has a new and exciting adventure in the life of your church!

It is suggested that a word of thanks ought to go out to every member who has responded to the Service Pledge program—either from the pulpit on a Sunday morning or by phone from council

members—or perhaps both. These commitments should be acknowledged in some fashion after Service Pledge Sunday.

Whether or not pledges are carried out throughout the following year should not be a great concern. Essentially, each member has made a Service Pledge to the church and to God. What should unfold, *will unfold*. The pastor and council members should act as facilitators rather than "overlords" or "scorekeepers."

God's blessings on a successful and enriching Service Pledge campaign!

St. John's Community Church

5008 Wilkerson Avenue
Nashville, Any State 30662 (150)555-3057

MAKE YOUR OWN UNIQUE MARK!
or
(Your Christmas Gift to St. John's)

Dear _____,

How would you like to have the opportunity to be the founder, creator, inventor, organizer, motivator, coordinator, instigator, energizer, the doer . . . whew! . . . how would you like to be the mastermind behind a new idea or program here at St. John's?

The opportunity will be yours on Christmas Sunday, December _____. On that morning, each of us will present our gift of service—our Service Pledge—to our church for _____ (year).

Just think of the possibilities! Is there, in your opinion, a void in our church ministry or programming that needs to be filled? Do you have a special talent that could be utilized somewhere in the church? Have you observed a continuing need here that remains unmet because it's no one's job to do it? Are there things that ought to be done, but never get done? Do we need to launch a new program? . . . put new life into a program that exists but just sort of limps along? . . . or resurrect a program that used to be but isn't anymore?

Is it time, dear friend, for YOU to answer the challenge—and make a new, different, and lasting contribution to St. John's?

Christmas Sunday is a ways off yet; therefore, you have a lot of time to think about what kind of Service Pledge you might make to the life of our parish in _____ (year). Put it on your mind's

back burner, but leave it on simmer. Give your Service Pledge to St. John's some serious thought. We want fresh ideas, new energy, creative and meaningful programs. Keep your eyes and ears open throughout the next several weeks—you'll be hearing much more about this new and exciting Service Pledge campaign for _____ (year).

For now, every young person and adult in our congregation should think about his or her answers to the following questions: What needs to be done in my church? How can I help get the job done? Or can I perhaps take the lead and find others to help me do the job?

Please give your Service Pledge to St. John's prayerful consideration.

With God's blessings,

Pastor Johnson

YOUR SERVICE TO YOUR CHURCH CAN MAKE A DIFFERENCE!

Have you ever said or thought the following?

What this church needs is . . .
I wish somebody would do something about . . .
I would love to see St. John's start . . .
Our church just doesn't have enough . . .
Why hasn't anyone in our church ever . . .

Were you able to complete all of the above statements?

You know what? You just may be the *somebody* in our church who can turn a good idea into a terrific reality! You may be the *leader* who can fill that vacancy, that empty chair, that unfilled slot. You. *You* just may be the answer to some of those unfinished statements above!

Think about it. Take an inventory of your ideas, talents, skills. How could you put them to use in your church? Where? When? How often?

Here's your chance to be an answer—a solution—to one of those unfinished statements. Service Pledge Sunday is December____. Service Pledge forms will be handed out in a special packet next Sunday. Please make sure you take one packet for each member in your family.

Pray about your Service Pledge to St. John's.

The greatest among you will be your servant.
(Matthew 23:11)

YOUR SERVICE TO YOUR CHURCH CAN MAKE A DIFFERENCE!

This morning, Service Pledge packets—including your Service Pledge form and special envelope—will be handed out at the doors following the service.

Please take one for yourself—and one for every young person and adult in your family.

Please read the material inside your packet carefully. Read and reread the Service Pledge form itself. Now is the time to start thinking about how YOU could make a vital and lasting contribution to your church.

> The church is a workshop, not a dormitory; and every Christian man and woman is bound to help in the common cause.
> —*Alexander MacLaren*

Each of us will have the opportunity to present our Service Pledge on Sunday, December___. We will bring them forward and lay them on the altar table. You may gift-wrap your Service Pledge, if you wish.

If you will not be here on Sunday, December___, please mail or deliver your Service Pledge to the church office. You may use the special envelope provided.

Pray about your Service Pledge to St. John's.

> We are worthless slaves; we have done only what we ought to have done! (Luke 17:10)

St. John's Community Church

5008 Wilkerson Avenue
Nashville, Any State 30662 (150)555-3057

Dear Fellow Member of St. John's,

Do you need help in deciding what kind of Service Pledge to make for _____ (year)? The following people serve as chairpersons for the many special work areas and age-level ministries in our church. If you see an area below that interests you—and you would like to know how you might contribute in that particular area of ministry—please feel free to call any of these chairpersons. They will be happy to hear from you and to offer some suggestions. They will also be glad to listen to your ideas.

Special Ministry	Chairperson	Home Phone
Christian Education		
Children's Ministries		
Junior High Ministries		
High School Ministries		
College Age Ministries		
Young Adult Ministries		
Adult Ministries		
Older Adult Ministries		
Family Ministries		
Stewardship		
Worship/Music/Arts		
Special Programs		
Church Camping		
Publicity/Newsletter		
Social Concerns		
Church Health/Welfare		
Evangelism/Outreach		
Missions		
Finance		
Church Property/Upkeep		
Other		

Remember, every member of your family is encouraged to make his or her own Service Pledge.

P. 2

Service Pledges will be presented on Christmas Sunday, December____. If you will not be in church that Sunday, please mail or deliver your Service Pledge to the church office before the year is out. Thank you for giving this special commitment much thought and prayer.

Pastor Johnson

SOME QUESTIONS AND ANSWERS ABOUT
THE SERVICE PLEDGE

Q: **What is a "Service Pledge"?**

A: A Service Pledge is a new idea. In fact, St. John's may be one of the first churches anywhere to launch a Service Pledge campaign. The Service Pledge gives *you* the opportunity to make a commitment of time and service to the church for 19— in whatever manner you choose. Your commitment can be big, small, long, short, a one-time project or a continuing program. And it is your golden opportunity to not only come up with a wonderful idea, but to help give that idea substance and shape! Hey, you wanna start something? HERE'S YOUR CHANCE!

Q: **What if I'm already giving time and service to the church?**

A: Great! Keep doing what you're doing. The Service Pledge gives you the chance to do something in addition—something new, different, unique— something urgently needed in our church. It's an opportunity for you to increase the giving of yourself to your church.

Q: **If I make a Service Pledge for 19— to St. John's—and fulfill my pledge, am I done? Is that all I have to do?**

A: That's up to you. But we certainly hope not. The Service Pledge is not meant to be a replacement for things you may already be doing in the church—and it certainly isn't meant to limit your church activity. It is merely a way of giving active members a chance to increase the giving of themselves—and to bring others into the mainstream of church ministry and programming. Some people are shy, and therefore are reluctant to step forward. The Service Pledge is a way to help them step forward and get involved. Others would like to do more, but they don't know where help is needed or where their special abilities could be used. The Service Pledge is designed to show where the needs are in all areas of ministry. The Service Pledge is a way to discover, recognize, and apply the special talents, skills, and interests of each young person and adult at St. John's. It's a way for YOU to make an important and lasting contribution to Christ's Church.

Q: **When do we make our Service Pledge?**

A: On Christmas Sunday, December ___, we will present our Service Pledges to the church. If you already know you will not be here that Sunday, please mail or deliver your Service Pledge to the church office.

Q: **Where do we get our Service Pledge forms?**

A: Service Pledge forms and special envelopes will be handed out the first three Sundays in December (___, ___, ___). You may pick yours up at the door following the worship hour. We encourage you to get yours early in the month so that you'll have a lot of time to read over the material and give your Service Pledge a great deal of thought and prayer.

Q: **Do I take just one Service Pledge form for my entire family?**

A: *No.* Each young person and adult in your family should have his or her own Service Pledge form and envelope. This is a pledge made by each adult and young person in our church. And both members and non-members are encouraged to make a Service Pledge. REMEMBER, TAKE ONE FOR EACH ADULT AND YOUNG PERSON IN YOUR FAMILY.

Q: **What if I don't wish to make a Service Pledge at this time?**

A: That's fine. No one is going to twist your arm to make your Service Pledge on Sunday, December ___. Your presence at St. John's is already a gift. It's good to have you in our fellowship. However, if you have a special talent, interest, skill, or ability of any kind—we encourage you to think seriously about how you might use it in service to your church. If you're only a little involved in the life of St. John's, we'd love to have you more involved! But it's your decision. And certainly, you may wait and make your Service Pledge later in the year if you're not ready now. (But pray about it and push yourself to take the step sooner rather than later.)

Q: **But I don't want to get stuck doing a project all by myself . . .**

A: You won't. That's why the Council on Ministries (C.O.M.) in our church will be very active in defining needs, enlisting assistants, and making sure that there is enough help to tackle a specific project or program. If you have a program or project that you would like to launch and organize, members of the C.O.M. will be happy to work with you to find needed funds, helpers, and additional support.

Q: **What if I want to make a Service Pledge, but I don't know what to give or how to get started?**

A: When you receive your Service Pledge envelope, you will find a list of our C.O.M. members inside. These people are the chairpersons of various work areas and ages in our church. They know the needs in their particular areas. Feel free to talk to any of them in person or by phone. AND REMEMBER, YOU MAY HAVE AN IDEA TO SHARE WITH THEM THAT THEY HAVE NEVER THOUGHT ABOUT BEFORE. Also, ask the minister for help and suggestions.

Best of all, talk to one another in the pews. The more we all communicate our concerns and dreams, the more we will generate exciting ideas and turn those ideas into program realities!

But just in case you haven't received your Service Pledge information yet, below are listed some examples of church involvement—just to help you in the thinking process. These are only suggestions. *Come up with your own ideas, too!*

EXAMPLES OF WORK AREAS	*POSSIBLE NEEDS & SERVICES*
1. Social Service/Health & Welfare/Community Service	1. Hospital/Shut-in visitation/Transporting the elderly to and from church/Assisting with home communion/etc.
2. Special Events/ Programs	2. Serve on special program committee/Assist with children's programs at rehearsals/Help with publicity/ etc.
3. Church Repair/ Maintenance	3. Greenery & landscaping upkeep (interior & exterior)/Repair broken nursery toys, tables, chairs/Painting/etc.
4. Christian Education	4. Teacher assistant/Summer Sunday school teacher/ Vacation Bible School helper /etc.
5. Worship/Prayer	5. Presider for worship/ Greeter/Choir/Start a prayer circle support group/ Help organize a Sunday "Coffee Fellowship"/etc.

MY SERVICE PLEDGE FOR 19—

(For every young person and adult in your family)

(Please fill out this Service Pledge form completely, then insert it in your special Service Pledge envelope and gift-wrap your pledge [if you wish] in any manner you choose. Make it as creative as you want! We will present our *gifts of service* to St. John's Community Church on Christmas Sunday morning, December___, during the worship celebration.)

1. Yes, I am making a Service Pledge to St. John's for _____ (period of time) in the area of: (If you're still not sure just how or where your time/service is needed, please refer to #6.)

    _____
    (your area of involvement)

2. Specifically, here's what I would like to do. (Please elaborate and use an extra sheet, if necessary.)

    _____
    _____
    _____
    _____

3. My particular service will be carried out over a period of:

    —one year (Jan.-Dec. _____)

    —the next six months (Jan.-June _____)

    —other (Please specify.) _____

4. The timing of my service will be in the form of:
   —a block of hours . . . Approximately how many hours? _____
   —a one-time project . . . Any specific time or date? _____
   —a project that will occur periodically throughout a given time period; such as weekly, monthly, quarterly, etc. (See below)
   Regarding the latter, please indicate the frequency timetable of your particular service:

   _____

5. After you have presented your pledge of service on Christmas Sunday morning, would you like:
   —to be called by someone on the C.O.M. to discuss the how and when of your service pledge.
   —not to be called. I would rather initiate the contact after additional thought and planning on my own.
   —Other _____

   _____

6. Yes, I want to make a Service Pledge to St. John's, but I am still not sure just how or where my help is needed. (Please check one or more of the following.)
   —Please assign me to help with a particular program or project that needs to be done.
   —My assignment may be in *any area* where help is needed.
   —I want to be assigned only in the following area (areas): _____; _____;
   _____; _____

—I would be interested in being a program or project *leader*.

—I would be interested in being a program or project *helper*.

—Please have someone on the C.O.M. call me to discuss my specific Service Pledge assignment.

(Please go back and fill in all other appropriate items.)

7. After I have fulfilled my pledge of service, I would be interested in:

—receiving another pledge form in the mail so that I could consider *renewing* my pledge (or changing it) for another time period.

—receiving a personal call or visit from a member of the C.O.M. to discuss my past and future contributions of service to St. John's.

—just taking it easy for a while to reflect on my past, present, and future service to St. John's.

—other _____

Thank You!

Your Name _____ Date _____

Address _____

Home Phone _____ Work Phone _____

(optional)

(REMINDER: PLEASE MAKE SURE EVERY YOUNG PERSON AND ADULT IN YOUR FAMILY HAS THE OPPORTUNITY TO MAKE A SERVICE PLEDGE.)

One final request: Depending on your response to this Service Pledge campaign, we may try it again next year. Please share any thoughts, suggestions, and comments you may have regarding this whole Service Pledge concept. Include these on a separate sheet of paper and enclose it with your Service Pledge in the envelope.

Your Service to Your Church Can Make a Difference!

Life is like a game of tennis;
the player who serves well seldom loses.
(Anonymous)

Sunday, December ___, is Service Pledge Sunday.

You still have a lot of time to think about what kind of time/service commitment you want to make to St. John's for _____ (year).

Service Pledge packets will be available at the doors this morning as you leave. If you haven't taken yours, please do so today—and please take one for every member of your family.

Still not sure what kind of pledge to make?

Don't hesitate to call any member of the Council on Ministries (C.O.M.). C.O.M. members and their work areas are listed in your Service Pledge packet. Ask them for ideas. They'll be glad to share suggestions—and listen to yours.

Imagine! Your Service Pledge to St. John's for _____ (year) just could be the start of something wonderful and exciting. Present your Service Pledge on Christmas Sunday, December ___.

Pray about your Service Pledge to St. John's.

Speak, Lord, for your servant is listening.
(I Samuel 3:9)

Your Service to Your Church Can Make a Difference!

Gifts come in many forms. Things. Companionship. Fellowship. Laughter. Time. Love. Service.

Next Sunday, each of us has the opportunity to give a Christmas gift of service to our church in the form of a Service Pledge. We will bring our Service Pledges to the altar table during the morning worship hour.

This is an important step for each of us. By making a Service Pledge to St. John's, we are saying: With God's help, I am willing and able to serve my church in a new and special way. I am ready to respond to a new challenge. I am ready to step forward and do my best.

Bless you as you make your Service Pledge for _____ (year). And may God bless our congregation as we strive to enhance and expand the ministry of Christ's Church.

It still isn't too late to pick up your Service Pledge packet. You may do so at the door this morning after the service.

If you will not be here next Sunday, please mail or deliver your Service Pledge to the church office.

Pray about your Service Pledge to St. John's.

A Letter to Write . . . and Then Shred!

Dear Church "Mover and Shaker" . . .

God loves you and so do I. But will you quit trying to run the church? I know you mean well
(don't you?). I know you miss the good ol' days
when Reverend So-and-So was here and let you
call the shots. But you know as well as I do that
Reverend So and So was incompetent, inept, and
intimidated by you and a few others. Well, I'm not,
and I'm not, and I'm not! So will you please forget
the past and join the rest of us in the present.
We're having a ball working together!

May God ~~bash~~ bless you.

Pastor Johnson

Aldersgate United Methodist Church

23 West Crescent Blvd., Denton, Any State 77443
Phone: (173)555-4323

Dear Church Member . . .

The season of Advent challenges us to fulfill John the Baptist's exhortation: "Prepare the way of the Lord" (Matthew 3:3). The word "Advent" means coming or arrival. In its basic meaning, it refers to the historical coming of Christ in human form. It also refers to the ascended Lord, who will return at the end of time as we know it to bring in the fullness of God's kingdom. Advent is the season to watch and wait—expectantly, joyfully. It is also the time to *make ready* for the coming of Jesus Christ.

Are we ready?

In this spirit of preparation, let us reflect on our readiness to receive the Lord. Have you and I kept our hearts open to Christ? Are we ready and willing to receive his transforming presence in our lives? As we prepare for Christ's birthday, are we preparing for our own personal rebirth?

As a church, have we maintained a state of preparedness? If Christ were to appear in our doorway during Advent, would we run toward or away from him? More important, would he walk in—or walk by? How have we—members of Aldersgate United Methodist Church—prepared the way of the Lord?

(Etc.)

Seasonal Letters

ADVENT/CHRISTMAS LETTER—INTRODUCTION / *167*

St. John's Community Church

5008 Wilkerson Avenue
Nashville, Any State 30662 (150)555-3057

Dear Church Family Member . . .

We are all so very busy. We are pushed and pulled every which way, seldom having the chance to catch our breath. While the upcoming Lenten season traditionally requires that we give up something in order to devote more time and energy to Christian service, we find it nearly impossible to do so.

Therefore, without asking you to fast for forty days or practice some other kind of abstinence, let me suggest that each of you focus your thoughts on the forty days that Jesus spent in the wilderness following his baptism (Matthew 4).

To most of us, having forty days alone in the tranquility of the outdoors would be heaven on earth. Cleansing. Revitalizing. And while it must have been restful for Jesus, too, it was also a period of trial and unsettledness. Jesus prayed a great deal while in the desert. He reflected on who he was. He thought about his earthly mission as set forth by his heavenly father. More than once he was confronted with temptation. But he resisted. He fortified his purpose and will.

Let us do the same this Lenten season. Let's each set aside some quiet time for prayer, meditation, and spiritual recommitment. Let's think about those things that steer us in the wrong direction, and let's renew our covenant with God to resist those things and fortify our hearts and minds with Christian purpose and intent.

(Etc.)

168 / LENTEN LETTER—INTRODUCTION

Dear Church Member . . .

Christ is risen! This proclamation isn't just an event that we celebrate on Easter Sunday. It is our Christian battle cry!

Christ is risen! Notice the present tense *is*. This isn't an event in the past. It is an ever-present happening that fuels our living and vibrant faith! Christ is alive and working through you and me! *Christ is! Right now! Hallelujah!*

The significance of the Resurrection as a historical event is simply incredible. It is the cornerstone of our spiritual substance. Christ's resurrection galvanized his reluctant, disbelieving disciples. Out of their disillusionment emerged a recommitted group who carried Christianity to the four corners of the world.

The importance of the Resurrection as a continuing event for today, tomorrow, and forever after is even more profound. It is victory over death. It is the promise of new life. And it is our commitment to share this extraordinary news to which each of us should rededicate ourselves this Easter season.

Christ is risen! Today! Tomorrow! Always! Even unto the end of the world! Hallelujah!

(Etc.)

Emmanuel Lutheran Church

107 Brook Dr.

Bethay

Any State 45789

(199)555-6811

Good Shepherd
Community Church

968 Honeysuckle Road
Breezeville, Any State   05050
Phone: (101)555-5467

Dear Church Member . . .

With the coming of the Pentecost season (or Ordinary Time, as it is sometimes called), we will enter into what might be called the "second semester" of the church year. Whereas the first half of the church year deals with Christ's birth, ministry, death, and resurrection, the long, non-festival Pentecost season emphasizes Christ's teachings and parables.

In John 14:18, Christ promises, "I will not leave you orphaned." He keeps that promise with the giving of the Holy Spirit to his disciples and to his new church. On Pentecost Sunday, therefore, we commemorate Christ's church unified in the Holy Spirit, empowered for its mission in the world. The gift of the Holy Spirit is God's way of continuing Christ's work on earth.

Pentecost is the time that we are to grow in the understanding of our Lord's teachings. It is the season during which we focus on applying Christianity to our daily living. After all the "Hosannas!" it is now time to put muscle on our faith and put it to work!

It is ironic that the long Pentecost season—the time of the church—includes the summer months when traditionally many of us go on extended vacations. I implore you not to allow the summer portion of Pentecost to become a kind of "spiritual hibernation." If we are truly to grow in the understanding of our Lord's teachings, then we cannot take a vacation from *living them*.

(Etc.)

A Letter to Write... and Then Shred!

Dear, Dear Parishioners...

We have the joy, joy, joy, joy in our hearts! We praise God from whom all blessings flow! We rejoice in the Lord and proclaim him to be a mighty fortress! Why then when we worship do we all look as if our dog died? Good grief. We look and act like we have a 50-pound anchor chained to our faith! When we sing, our mouths mouth words like joy, praise, spirit, celebrate, and glory. But our faces say bland, dull, boring, humdrum, and yawn.

Do any of us really listen to what we're singing or reciting or praying? Has habit really become such a deadener that we merely open our bulletins and turn ourselves on "automatic pilot"—reacting blankly to an order of stimuli rather than an order of service? Have liturgy and lethargy become interchangeable? Huh? Huh? Hey, anybody out there?

Dear God, what have we done to our faith?

Pastor Johnson

St. John's Community Church

5008 Wilkerson Avenue
Nashville, Any State 30662 (150)555-3057

Dear . . .

A foreigner who was learning English defined "fellowship" as "fellows in the same ship." As I prepare to leave my parish here at St. John's Community Church, I have reflected on our many good times together. We have accomplished some fine things in this community, working as brothers and sisters of the faith in Christ's holy name. Indeed, we have served as brothers and sisters on the same ship.

I am making this change of my own accord for both personal and professional reasons. I have always asked God to use me according to his will and purpose. I believe I am responding to his call.

May God continue to shine his blessings upon your lives as you carry out his work. My friends, (I/we) will miss you and your families. Thank you for your friendship and love.

With love and gratitude,

Pastor Johnson

CENTRAL BAPTIST CHURCH

Route 66   Longville,   Any State   98989
(111)555-3879

Dear . . .

As you know by now, (I am/my family and I are)
preparing to leave (my/our) ministry at Central
Baptist Church. It is hard to say goodbye. How can
(I/we) express how much all of you have meant to
(me/us) over the years? It has been a pleasure
working and planning with you. But most of all, it
has been sheer delight just knowing you and sharing the joys of our faith together!

Albert Schweitzer once said, "Sometimes our
light goes out but is blown into flame by an
encounter with another human being. Each of us
owes the deepest thanks to those who have rekin-
dled this inner light."

My deepest thanks to all of you, dear friends.
Thank you for your inspiration and light. May you
continue to enrich one another for the glory of the
one who is the Light of all life.

Blessings upon you.

Pastor Johnson

Emmanuel Lutheran Church

107 Brook Dr.

Bethay

Any State 45789

(199)555-6811

Dear . . .

I am writing to inform you that I will be resigning my pastorate at Emmanuel Lutheran Church, effective _____ (date). I owe you the courtesy of letting you know before it becomes common knowledge.

Resigning from a job, no matter what the reason, is never easy. It's even more difficult when a person must say goodbye to such an outstanding staff and wonderful friends. You have been a source of inspiration to me. My ministry here would not have been nearly as effective or rewarding without your help.

There's no need to go into specifics at this time. I will share more with each of you when the time and circumstances deem it appropriate. Suffice it to say that it is time for a change, for new direction and greater challenges. God has been speaking to me, but only recently did he get my undivided attention. I have prayed that his will be done. He is responding, and I am now listening.

Bless you for all that you have done for me and for this great church. There is still work to be done. I pray that you will carry on as good and faithful servants of God.

Thank you for being you.

With much love,

Pastor Johnson

Good Shepherd Community Church

968 Honeysuckle Road
Breezeville, Any State   05050
Phone: (101)555-5467

Dear . . .

Please accept this letter as a personal word to each of you from (me/me and my family). Effective _____ (date), I will be appointed pastor of _____ (church), in _____ (location).

Good Shepherd Community Church truly has been home for (me/us). You have nurtured (me/us) with your friendship and love. You have helped our children grow and mature spiritually. As I reflect on the prospect of relocating, I also affirm in my heart that Good Shepherd Community Church will always remain ("my church"/"our church"). A lasting bond has been forged by all that we have shared together. Although (I am/we are) leaving you soon, you will always have a special place in (my heart/our hearts), as (I/we) trust (I/we) will have in yours.

God calls us on the journey to our ultimate home. As (I/we) prepare to leave and you ready yourselves to welcome a new pastor, let us all pray that we will be sensitive to God's presence and even more responsive to God's guidance. By being drawn more closely to God, we will be drawn even more closely together.

There will be time for personal farewells later. Let this word be enough for now.

Grace and peace.

In Christ,

Pastor Johnson

A Letter to Write . . . and Then Shred!

Dear Parishioner,

Contrary to popular belief, there is no large S on my shirt underneath my alb. Only coffee drips and sweat stains.

Give me a break. I'm only human.

In gratitude,

Pastor Johnson